Supernatural
Liverpool

Published by The Bluecoat Press, Liverpool
Book design by March Design, Liverpool
Printed by Design 2 Print

Cover picture, Picton Clock, Wavertree

ISBN 1 872568 74 2

Supernatural
Liverpool

Billy Roberts

The Bluecoat Press

Contents

Foreword by Tom Slemen

I clearly remember my life as a child, way back in the 1970s, when I lived in Myrtle Street, close to Liverpool city centre. Back in those golden days of my boyhood, I can recall how one day I wandered into terra incognita, the unchartered neighbourhood somewhere in the direction of the Bullring tenements off Brownlow Hill - the edge of my known world. I met a lad from that area who was looking at a comic which featured someone who was to become one of my greatest heroes: Doctor Strange.

"What's that you're reading," I asked, cautiously sidling up to him to get a closer look.

"Erm, Strang-le or something," he mumbled, trying to sound casual but obviously having difficulty reading even the title of the comic.

I was immediately captivated by what I could see of the Doctor Strange character from where I was standing.

"Swap you a packet of Maltesers and a tube of Swizzlers for it," I ventured, assuming, correctly as it turned out, that they would be of more use to him than a comic which he clearly could not read.

"OK," he agreed, "I've already finished it anyway."

By the time that I had walked back home, I had read the comic from cover to cover and a new influence had entered my life; a new hero, besides Spider Man and the Incredible Hulk.

The Doctor Strange comic book series, created by Stan Lee, the Hans Christian Andersen of the jet age, told an imaginative tale of a self-centred and materialistic surgeon who injured his hands in a car accident. In an effort to heal them, Dr Stephen Strange sought out a powerful magician in the Himalayas. The mighty magician ended up repairing Strange's soul, as well as his hands. After learning to set aside his selfishness, Strange became the magician's apprentice, which put him at dire odds with Baron Mordo, an earlier evil apprentice.

Over the course of time (and many comic books), Strange became the Sorcerer Supreme and set up headquarters in New York's exotic and bohemian Greenwich Village, where he guarded Earth from supernatural forces and Mordo's determination to destroy him. Strange also battled against wicked wizards as well as more abstract enemies such as Nightmare and Eternity; in each encounter his weapon was knowledge rather than brute force.

I loved the misunderstood Hulk, especially the television version, who had the unshakeable Mr McGee on his tail, because the school inspector on the trail of the young truant, Tom Slemen, was also a Mr McGee. Doctor Strange, however, appealed to me because of the amazing concepts. Strange could levitate with his cloak, he could project his astral body anywhere and had ready access to other dimensions, void spaces and mystical planes unknown to mere mortals. He had the infamous

Necronomican and other fabulous books in his vast library of esoterica and could even access data from an immense information lattice (which would dwarf the internet), called the Akashic Records. I later learned that many of the concepts contained in these amazing Marvel comic books were rooted in real occult lore. That made me wonder; could there be real Doctor Stranges at large in the world; dedicated masters and practitioners of the occult science? More intriguing still: could I become a Doctor Strange?

I read as much as I could on the subject of the occult and realised that, without a doubt, there was, in the dim remote past, an epoch when a great civilisation reached its zenith. The scientific knowledge of that ancient time was developed to a point where it became indistinguishable from what we would now categorise as magic and things are now moving in the same direction again. We have everyday computers which can understand and translate speech and no one even bats an eyelid. We can transplant hearts and lungs and scientists have even successfully transplanted the heads of monkeys and dogs, yet no one is surprised by such feats anymore.

As I write, an American who tragically lost his 10-year-old daughter is asking geneticists to clone her. He has been told it is entirely possible, but legislation has not caught up with science yet, so those in the field have to tread very carefully. We have become very blasé about breakthroughs today.

Even in the last century, after two men were put down on the moon, the novelty and excitement of lunar exploration soon wore off. This has all happened before. No one likes to use the word impossible any more, because, like hackers, someone always finds a way through a technical obstacle. It used to be the sound barrier; now it is the light barrier. Where will this relentless progress end? I say in magic. Inside our brains there are mysterious dormant areas which continue to puzzle neurologists. These brain sections obviously serve some purpose, but no one knows what that purpose is.

Our brains are like high-octane Grand Prix racing cars, stuck in a slow-moving traffic jam; we crawl along and the speedometer needle never moves beyond a snail's pace. One day, though, when we have pushed our machines and electronic hardware to the absolute limit, we will turn our attention to the complexities of the human mind. Some people, such as psychologists and what we call psychics, have already started to explore the world of the human mind. One person who has made headway in that direction is Billy Roberts.

When I first met Billy Roberts, I was surprised. I had ignorantly assumed that he was a typical, run-of-the-mill medium who had no real interest in the spirit world; just a determination to make a fast buck out of duping vulnerable old people into thinking that they were having messages relayed to them from their loved ones. But I was wrong. My generalisation was formed from my own experiences of seeing shameless charlatans operating under the guise of psychics.

Billy Roberts possesses a unique attribute which is very rare today: honesty. I once took him to an old building in Liverpool with a reputation for being haunted and asked him what was coming through, his reply was: "To tell you the truth, Tom, I'm not picking up anything at all."

On other occasions he has homed in on entities with startling results. A case in point is the night he was on Pete Price's radio phone-in show, on Magic 1548. A woman asked him if she had any messages from the a loved one who had passed on. Billy gave her a message and did something most mediums never do: he produced the surname of the person he had made contact with. This was later verified by the caller, who was astonished by his abilities. That is just one of the many weird incidents which I have experienced around Billy Roberts.

Billy is the nearest person to the character of Doctor Strange in my eyes. He is mild-mannered, well-spoken and very focused. He uses esoteric terms and his speech is routinely peppered with conceptual terms from Buddhism and Shamanism. He uses Celtic and Sanskrit words when he is philosophising about latent human powers and hidden faculties, which would leave an Oxford professor scratching his pate. In a matter-of-fact way he describes how to scry and glimpse beyond the curtain of present time, as if he is telling you how to set the video recorder. I have never met a person as open-minded to the possibilities of the human mind as Billy Roberts. He is a true scholar of the occult; a dedicated savant of the supernatural and it is always a pleasure to read what he writes.

Within this volume, Billy relates some fascinating and intriguing tales and I hope that you will enjoy them as much as I did.

Introduction

I have come to the conclusion that everyone has at least one eerie tale to tell. Most people have had, at some time or another, some sort of ghostly or paranormal experience and even the so-called sceptic has to admit to being a little more than curious about the supernatural.

During the course of my 25 years as a professional medium and paranormal investigator, I have found myself in more than one frightening situation, in which I have been certain that my life was in danger. It is quite easy for me to look back, with hindsight, in an effort perhaps to convince myself that there was no real danger and I was not really afraid at the time. However, the truth is that, even with my knowledge and experience as a medium, I can still feel fear, particularly when the experience is beyond my control. Poltergeists and things that go bump in the night are commonplace in my work as a paranormal investigator, but there have been rare occasions when I have found myself confronted with spontaneous paranormal activity and have not really had time to determine exactly what was happening to me, or to plan a course of action.

I can recall one such experience when I was called to a Victorian house, in Birkdale, in which the occupants had complained of poltergeist activity. The house was situated in the same road as the famous Palace Hotel and so I welcomed the invitation with some excitement.

However, my complacent attitude was shaken as soon as I walked through the heavy Victorian door and into the wide hallway. I was immediately overwhelmed by the pungent aroma of damp earth and smouldering rags, a smell which I had experienced many times before and which I had come to associate with poltergeists and discarnate vagabonds. The anxious owner of the house explained that some invisible force was causing havoc and devastation to his home. The phenomenon had begun when he first moved into the house four years before and the whole paranormal scenario had caused a great deal of distress, financially and otherwise, to the family as a whole. He had made every effort to sell the old house but its reputation prevented any sale from being successful.

He left me to roam freely around and my curiosity led me slowly up the broad Victorian staircase and, as I did so, I felt a hand on my back and I turned around, expecting to find the owner of the house. However, instead, my eyes met a tall elderly gentleman, dressed in a long black Victorian-style overcoat. For a moment I thought that he was someone who lived in the house and I was just about to greet him, when he disappeared without trace. Unfazed by the experience, I turned round and continued to ascend the stairs. When I had reached the top, I was pushed roughly to one side by some invisible force. I could hear laughter and a child crying and then a small mahogany table began to glide slowly across the highly-polished floor of the landing, without disturbing the vase which had been placed upon it.

The owner of the house had given me total freedom to roam around his home and I felt instinctively guided towards one particular room along the dimly-lit corridor. Before I had even taken my first step towards it, my body suddenly became icy cold and I felt completely disorientated. At first I thought that I was going to faint but, instead, I felt my whole body being lifted from the floor. For at least 30 seconds I was suspended about four inches in the air and I felt as though I was completely paralysed. No one would ever have believed me, if the owner had not appeared at the top of the stairs at that moment, to witness the whole amazing scenario. He, however, was not at all surprised by what he saw, for he claimed that this phenomenon was commonplace in his Victorian home.

No sooner had I been lowered gently back down to the floor, than I vomited uncontrollably and, with great embarrassment, made my excuses to leave. Although I did return several times, I know that the old house was eventually demolished and a new building was erected in its place. I am convinced, however, that the old house may well have physically disappeared but the psychic structure of it still remains and the paranormal activity will most certainly continue. I, for one, will not be tempted to return.

Stories such as this one become far more real when we experience them for ourselves. We can never be one hundred per cent certain of the reality of the things around us and, even as you read this, someone may be watching you ...

Billy Roberts

The Little Girl with Pigtails

Even though the German bombers were systematically devastating the city of Liverpool in 1942, the spirit of the people and their instinct for survival remained strong and undaunted. Visible signs of the War were apparent everywhere and there was not a street, or even a single house, which did not bear the scars. In fact, in many areas, only desolation could be seen and the war-scarred streets of Wavertree, where Ken Luxton was born and had lived all his life, stood as a reminder that the whole country was under siege and was being savagely attacked by a ruthless nation which sought only to take control.

On one particularly awful night, bombs had fallen more or less constantly and had devastated houses in Ash Grove, Ashfield and Wavertree Vale. Ken Luxton had been helping to search for survivors in the debris of a house in Ash Grove, where he also lived, and had stopped to drink a welcome cup of tea, which was being served by a group of locals at the roadside. He stood pensively in complete silence, his eyes solemnly scanning the desolation before him, in horror and disbelief, only vaguely aware of the sounds around him, when he felt someone tugging insistently at his arm. He lowered his eyes to see a little girl with pigtails in her hair and the biggest pair of blue eyes that he had ever seen. She was crying hysterically and pulling at his arm, in an attempt to get him to follow her.

"Hang on there a minute, love," said Ken, kindly, stooping down to speak to her at her own height. "Now then, dry those eyes and tell me what's wrong."

"My mummy's trapped in the basement of our house," she sobbed. "Please help her. She can't move!"

"Right," said Ken, "but first of all, tell me your name."

"Linda," she replied, "Linda Graham."

"Ok, Linda," he continued. "My name's Ken. Show me exactly where your mummy is and we'll have her out in no time."

Without saying another word, the little girl sped off through the debris at the corner of Ash Grove, pausing for a moment to make sure that Ken was close behind. He followed her into the entry at the back of the corner grocer's shop and along another entry leading into Wavertree Vale. She stopped abruptly by the remains of what had once been a house at the corner of the entry and urgently beckoned Ken to the spot. He could see immediately that the building had been reduced to rubble in the previous night's air raid and he doubted if anyone could possibly have survived such an impact.

"She's in there," cried the little girl. "My mummy's trapped in the basement with Laddie, my doggie. Please help her. Please get her out."

Ken paused for a moment whilst his eyes surveyed the devastation before him and, despite his pessimistic assessment of the situation, he tried to reassure her.

"Don't worry, love, your mummy will be alright. We'll get her out. You just stand over there."

He picked his way cautiously towards the entrance to the basement of the house, scrambling over the bricks and debris, pausing for a moment to check that the little girl was at a safe distance. He could see that she was waiting anxiously at the roadside and so he continued to claw his way forward. There was no question that the house had taken a direct hit, which usually meant no survivors and Ken's task seemed almost futile, but he knew that he just had to continue for Linda's sake.

It was obvious that he needed help to clear the bricks and huge slabs of concrete that were blocking his way into the basement of the house, but time was of the essence if there was to be any hope of a successful rescue. Losing all track of time, he dug furiously and completely forgot about the little girl. As the minutes turned into hours, his clothes became stuck to his body with sweat and he ached so much that he felt as though he was about to collapse. But, just when he thought that he could continue no longer, he detected a muffled voice coming from beneath the rubble. He held his breath and stopped digging for a moment to listen, but all that he could hear was the occasional sound of falling bricks and cracking wood. He was just about to resume his efforts, when he heard the voice again.

"Please, please, help me …"

He lowered his ear to the place where he thought the sound was coming from and then yelled as loudly as he could.

"Keep shouting!" he urged. "Keep shouting so that I can work out exactly where to dig."

"Please help me," came the woman's voice. "Help me!"

The voice seemed to get louder each time it called and, with each call, Ken Luxton gathered more and more strength. Within minutes, he had somehow cleared a way into the basement and had pulled the woman and the dog clear of the rubble and out into the daylight. Although very badly shaken and more than a little bruised, Linda's mother was basically unharmed and was hugely relieved to see Ken's smiling face and to be out in the fresh air once again.

"Thank God!" she gasped, as he helped her to pick her way unsteadily over the rubble to the pavement. "Thank God you saved me. How on earth did you know I was down there?"

Ken laughed, overcome with emotion and understandable pride at his life-saving achievement.

"Nobody would ever have known you were there, if it hadn't been for your little girl!" and he smiled broadly and turned to look for Linda.

"Little girl?" said the woman, puzzled. "What little girl?"

"Your little girl," retorted Ken, suddenly wondering if she might have been concussed in the bombing.

"What did she look like?" asked the woman, obviously confused.

"Oh, about so high," said Ken indicating the little girl's height with his hand. "She had two pigtails and the biggest blue eyes I've ever seen. She said her name was

Linda."

A tear suddenly trickled down the woman's cheek, cutting a little river through the dust and grime which covered her from top to toe and the little girl's name fell almost silently from her lips.

"Linda!" she whispered, a slight trembling smile parting her lips. "My little Linda. She was killed in the first twelve months of the war."

"But I saw her with my own eyes" insisted Ken. "I actually spoke to her and touched her."

"My Linda!" repeated the woman. "My poor little girl ..."

The Murder of Samuel Feldon

It was Christmas Eve, 1798 and, as was usual every night at 8pm prompt, old Samuel Feldon, the shoemaker in the little village of Wavertree, pulled the bolt across the door of his shop with a contented sigh - another long day's work was finally over. He then made his way over to the counter, where he kept the day's takings in an old wooden box.

Watched by his apprentice, 16-year-old Mathew Gibbin, old Samuel placed the box on top of the counter, slowly turned the key and pulled back the lid. Peering at young Mathew over the top of his gold-rimmed spectacles, he retrieved three golden guineas from inside the box and placed them ceremoniously on the top of the scratched wooden surface of the counter.

"There you are, Mathew lad," he mumbled under his breath, somewhat embarrassed by his sudden burst of unaccustomed generosity. "There's your wages. Oh, and a little bonus on top."

"Three guineas!" gasped Mathew. "But ..."

"It's Christmas, boy," Samuel interrupted him, somewhat sharply. "You've been a good help to me over the years. I dare say you could do with a little extra money now that you are the man of the house. Now, be off with you, before I change my mind, your mother will be waiting for you."

Young Mathew was hardly able to believe his luck and he eagerly scooped the three gold coins from the top of the counter and hurriedly put on his coat. He was wrapping his woollen scarf carefully around his neck, when he turned at the door to thank the old man and bid him a final farewell.

"Good night, Mr Feldon. Thankyou very much for my bonus and a Merry Christmas to you."

"Be off, boy," he snapped, not wanting to show any more sentiment than he had done already.

Mathew was quite bemused by the whole affair, which was totally out of character for his employer, so he pulled back the bolt on the door and opened it, ready to make a quick exit before he changed his mind.

"Good night, Mr Feldon," he ventured, one last time, before disappearing into the cold December night.

Samuel Feldon was not a generous man. In fact, everyone knew him as an old skinflint. Mathew Gibbin had worked for him since his father, Ned, had died three years before, when he had just turned thirteen. The responsibility for looking after his mother and three young sisters was now on his young shoulders and, together, they lived in a little rented cottage, in nearby Mill Lane. Mathew counted himself as being very lucky to be working at all in such impoverished times and, although old Samuel Feldon was not the easiest man to work for, he thoroughly enjoyed his job as an apprentice shoemaker and hoped that one day he would have his own, similar business.

Although nobody knew for certain, old Samuel Feldon was thought to be quite wealthy. He lived in a modest little house in Olive Lane with his spinster sister, Margaret and her two cats. Because he and his sister had always kept themselves to themselves, no one knew very much about them. Margaret attended the local church every Sunday morning without fail and Samuel would occasionally be seen calling in to the nearby Lamb Inn for one gill of beer, before wending his way slowly back home along Mill Lane.

As soon as the young apprentice had left, old Samuel secured the bolt on the door and proceeded to count the day's takings into his pouch, which he then pushed neatly into his inside coat pocket. After checking that his shop was completely secure, Samuel put on his heavy winter coat and threw his scarf around his neck. He extinguished the two oil lamps at either side of the shop, pulled back the bolt and fully opened the door to face the sharp winter wind outside. He closed the door firmly behind him and carefully turned the key in the lock, a ritual which he had repeated for the past 50 years, then he turned to make his way across the High Street towards Mill Lane. Although he was an extremely cautious man, he was also a creature of habit and strict routine. He was ever vigilant in the hard and often wicked times and was only too aware that many people in the locality resented the fact that he was quite comfortably off and liked to keep to himself.

Despite his 75 years, he was quite sprightly and looked extremely young for his years. On this particular evening he had reached the turning into Olive Lane in no time at all but was beginning to feel the night chill in his aching bones. Thinking that he had detected a figure lurking in the shadows, old Samuel paused for a moment by the trees.

"Who's there?" he called.

But his question met only silence. It was a moonlit night and the swaying branches of the trees cast crazy, dancing shadows across his path. The sharp wind whipped against his face and distracted his attention for a moment, then an aggressive voice called out sharply to him from the gloom.

"We want your money, Feldon. Let us have your money and you won't get hurt."

Old Samuel's heart quickened against his ribs, as his aged eyes scoured the darkness for the source of the voice. Suddenly he noticed a movement in some bushes and he could make out three shadowy figures emerging from the darkness.

"Give us your money, old man," repeated one of the figures approaching Samuel.

Samuel was not a particularly brave man but he was no coward either.

"You'll get no money from me," he announced adamantly, whilst inwardly trembling and turning to walk away, his steps suddenly quickening as his anxiety mounted. He did not get very far, as his way was immediately barred by one of the burly figures, who callously punched the old man to the ground.

Samuel had noticed that, although there were three men, one of them kept his distance, as though not wanting to be recognised. As one of his attackers stooped to search his pockets for the money, the old man bravely tried to defend himself and pushed him away with all the strength he could muster. This act of defiance only served to anger the thug even more and he punched him once again, even more viciously. This further act of violence caused the anonymous figure to step out from the shadows.

"Take it easy, Joe," he urged, "you don't want to kill him, do you?"

Although he was disorientated by his ordeal, Samuel's eyes managed to bring the third man into focus.

"I know you!" he cried out, in a weak voice, pointing an accusing finger at the figure. "You're Tom Westley's lad."

Samuel's recognition of him brought a sharp, cold response.

"You'll have to do for him now, Joe! Finish him off, or we'll all go to prison."

The man standing over old Samuel immediately pulled a knife from his belt and plunged it deep inside his chest and, within moments, he was dead! After rifling through his pockets for the money, the murderous gang sped off into the darkness of Olive Lane.

The body was discovered, just before midnight, by a young couple returning from the village. But, because the following day was Christmas, nothing was actually done about the murder until Boxing Day.

The first person to be questioned by the local constabulary, was young Mathew Gibbins. The three golden guineas were quickly found in the Gibbins' household and the explanation as to how he had received them, met with complete and utter disbelief. Samuel Feldon was a known miser and the very idea of him giving anyone three golden guineas, as a gesture of goodwill, sounded completely absurd and was rejected out of hand. As far as the authorities were concerned, the case was cut and dried. Mathew Gibbins was guilty and would be tried for murder as soon as the festive season was over.

With his hands bound tightly behind him and accompanied by a jeering crowd, the young lad was marched to the lock-up at the top of the High Street, where he was to remain until the local judge could be summoned to hear the case. However, events soon took a very different turn and the legal process was denied to the accused. The locals decided that an example had to be made of Mathew Gibbins, whom they had branded as a thug and a murderer and they took it upon themselves to set up a vigilante committee in the judge's absence. The lock-up was raided on the evening after Christmas and the accused lad was taken to a nearby farm, without any further questions and hanged from a makeshift gibbet. He proclaimed his innocence until the very end and, with his very last breath, pleaded for mercy with those responsible for his hanging.

As instructed by the authorities, Mathew's body was taken by his family and friends to be buried in an unmarked grave at the edge of the village and very few people actually knew the whereabouts of his final resting place.

Emma Birch, a close family friend, discovered something quite unusual whilst taking a casual walk across the Abbey Common one sunny afternoon. Pausing to place some wild flowers at the spot where Mathew's body lay, she noticed a perfect cross of purple grass marking the site of the grave. Because nothing else grew upon the ground where his body had been laid to rest, the news quickly spread about the phenomenon of the purple cross and, of course, there was a lot of conjecture as to the possible reason for its appearance. Some claimed that it was a symbol to bring Mathew Gibbins peace and others were convinced that it was a sign of his innocence. But, whatever, or whoever, was responsible for the purple cross, for Mathew Gibbins it was too late ... or was it?

Samuel Feldon's shop is still standing, to this day, at the top of the High Street and it is now an antique shop. The lock-up is also still there, opposite what used to be the Abbey Cinema. The site of Mathew Gibbins' grave is thought to be where the children's swings are now situated, in Mill Lane. It is claimed by some of the present day locals, that his ghost can be sometimes seen, on Boxing Day, sitting on the step of the old lock-up, crying out for his mother.

The Mystery of Old Flynn

As the bells of Saint Margaret's, on the corner of Sheil Road, rang out to welcome in the new year of 1890, tea and cake was already being handed out to everyone who came through the doors of Belmont Road Workhouse. Although they were an impoverished and quite pitiful sight, all those present joined in the merriment of the occasion and prayed silently for a better and more prosperous new year. Workhouse attendant, John McBane, however, was not convinced that the prospects of the paupers would improve and was quite convinced, in his own mind, that their prayers would be exactly the same at this time next year. At least, though, they had hope and, with that, they had his full support, even though his prayers for them were somewhat different from those they said for themselves.

Of all the visitors to the shelter, old Flynn was somehow the odd one out. His erect, slender frame towered a good six feet four inches over the comparatively diminutive sizes of everyone else. He was well-spoken and extremely articulate and had obviously been well-educated in his youth, having the ability to speak knowledgeably on most subjects. He wore a thick, neat beard, which grew almost up to his large and happy brown eyes and his long, abundant grey hair fell loosely about his shoulders, giving him an almost biblical appearance.

John McBane liked old Flynn, even though he found him to be somewhat of a mystery. Over the months, his interest in him had deepened and he became increasingly suspicious of his true identity. Ordinarily he would have accepted his presence at the workhouse without question, had it not been for the fact that he exhibited some very unusual and extraordinary abilities.

Unaware that he was being observed, he was often seen laying his hands on the head of one of the workhouse occupants who was unwell, as if in an effort to administer some form of spiritual healing. This, in fact, was a common occurrence and, as medical care was extremely scarce, if not non-existent, for the poor in those difficult times, many of them turned to old Flynn when they were sick, having no other alternative.

He would occasionally be seen handing out small bottles containing an infusion of herbs and berries. His reputation quickly spread throughout the poverty-stricken areas of Victorian Liverpool, as some sort of healer and mystic and the sick came from all over the region to seek the old man's help. In fact, old Flynn brought a great deal of comfort to many people and some were apparently completely cured of their maladies after his ministrations.

Driven by his curiosity, John McBane decided to look out for an opportunity to follow him back to wherever it was that he returned each night. It was two days into the new year and Flynn had called into the workhouse to lend a hand with some cleaning and the serving of meals. John McBane had set his plan carefully in his mind and waited for Flynn to leave. The clock in the hall struck 11pm and, almost simultaneously, old Flynn readied himself to leave, as he nearly always did, more or less at the same time.

Upon leaving the workhouse, he paused for a moment at the corner of Belmont Road and West Derby Road, unaware that he was being followed. It was a busy night, with carriages and people making their way home and John McBane had to be keenly vigilant in his pursuit of old Flynn. The old man suddenly started to make his way along West Derby Road; his quickening pace making it almost impossible for his pursuer to keep up. The night was extremely dark, with scarcely any moon or starlight to illuminate their path and John McBane had to watch very carefully, to avoid losing sight of the old man's sprightly form.

It was approaching midnight and they had covered a fair distance and, by now, old Flynn had reached the vicinity of Woolton Road, not far from the village and had turned sharply through the gates leading into the gardens of what appeared to be an old manor house. McBane followed him as far as the gates and watched him ascend the stone steps and finally disappear through the heavy, ornate doors.

Peering through the darkness, at the sign above the high sandstone wall, John was surprised to read that the building in front of him was Saint Joseph's Monastery. Not quite knowing what to make of the discovery, he turned around and made his way back home.

Over a week had gone by and old Flynn had not been seen at the workhouse, or by any of the people who lived there, or regularly attended it. Thinking this was too much of a coincidence, John McBane decided to pay the monastery a visit the following afternoon. Upon being introduced to the Abbot, John told him the whole story from beginning to end. The priestly figure sat for a few moments in silence, observing John's anticipation and wondering exactly what the inquirer thought he might discover. Then, raising his eyes with a sigh, he rose to his feet and beckoned him to the window overlooking the beautiful gardens at the rear of the monastery.

"Old Flynn, you say?" he muttered, thoughtfully. He then gestured once again for him to look through the window. "There's your old Flynn!"

John peered curiously through the window to see two monks tending the flower beds, one of whom was unmistakably old Flynn.

"A monk?" muttered John McBane in disbelief. "Old Flynn is a monk?"

"Brother Francis!" corrected the Abbot with a smile. "Our own Brother Francis!"

Old Flynn was never seen again at the Liverpool Workhouse, but it was later discovered that he was known to have visited many other such places for the poor all over the Liverpool area. Some reports even claimed that he had also visited workhouses as far afield as Manchester and even London.

Steps up to the Church

It is a comforting idea to think that someone, somewhere, is watching over us and that when we are at our lowest ebb, that someone will always come to our rescue.

Dave Monroe had come to the point in his life where he found it very difficult to get through the day without some form of artificial substance to sustain him. Life had become unbearable because of drugs and now he felt so alone that he just wanted to die. He had no friends left and was keenly aware that he had let his family down. All his dreams and aspirations had come to nothing and now he spent most of his days wandering aimlessly through the streets of Wavertree, alone, waiting for the night to come, so that he could find comfort and peace in sleep. However, sleep offered no real refuge for him because, even then, he was quite often pursued by the self-created demons of his own mind. He was in such a state of despair, that he had now decided that death was the only answer to his never-ending nightmare.

It was the 1960s; supposedly the time of love, peace and transcendental meditation. From Dave Monroe's perspective, everyone around him seemed to be happy and liberated, whilst he was feeling empty and depressed. In a final effort to seek some sort of consolation and comfort, he wandered into Saint Hugh's Church, at the corner of Cramborne Road and Lawrence Road. Apart from an old lady kneeling silently in prayer before the altar, the church was empty and, more importantly to Dave, the atmosphere was peaceful and serene. Although he was not a Catholic, he had been in the church several times before, just to sit quietly and collect his thoughts. It had worked for him on those occasions and so he secretly hoped that the tranquillity which always seemed to pervade the church, would somehow take away his mental anguish and pain and convince him, once and for all, that death was not the answer.

He sat in his usual place, on the right hand side of the altar, as close to the wall as possible, so as not to be too conspicuous should anyone else come in. For several moments he just watched the old woman praying. The whole atmosphere in the church seemed to be charged with emotion and he found it difficult to contain his sadness any longer. He lowered his head in order to hide his tears and silence his sobs, which seemed to echo and multiply through the huge empty spaces of the religious edifice. But even the old woman paid no attention to him and she eventually rose to her feet and wended her way along the aisle, pausing for a moment to look back at the altar and respectfully bow her head. As she passed Dave, their eyes met for a brief moment and, in that moment, they shared the same sadness and pain. Although he kept facing the front of the church, he could hear the door swing open and then close heavily as she left the church.

Silence once again returned to the whole building and even Dave's thoughts seemed to echo as they swirled around inside his head. No longer afraid of being heard, he sobbed loudly and prayed with all the energy and determination he could muster in his confused and distressed heart. When he had cried out all his tears, he sat in silence once again. He felt numb and empty inside and was only vaguely aware of his surroundings. Suddenly he sensed somebody watching him and turned to see a tall, elderly priest standing in the aisle at the end of his pew.

"I'm sorry if I startled you," said the priest with a broad Irish accent. "Would you like to talk to me?"

At first, Dave declined the offer and began to move as though he was getting ready to leave.

"I'm sorry!" continued the priest, "I've disturbed you. Please don't leave on my account. You're very welcome here. Stay as long as you want."

His voice was warm and reassuring and Dave needed so much to pour his heart out to someone. So he sat down again on the pew and the priest came and sat down quietly beside him. The priest encouraged him to unburden himself and then listened patiently while Dave told his whole sorry story from beginning to end. When he had finished, he looked expectantly at the priest in the hope of some sort of response, but none was given. In fact, a few uncomfortable moments elapsed as the priest stared thoughtfully at him in silence.

"Well then, my son!" he finally began. "I'm quite certain that your problems ended with the steps up to the church," and he touched Dave's hand, before making the sign of the cross. "God bless you, my son. God bless you!"

As Dave digested these words, the elderly priest rose and made his way along the aisle, towards the door at the rear of the church. After a short while, Dave turned round to look back at him, but he had gone.

It took Dave Monroe all of two months to contemplate his future and pull himself back together. Although he had said very little, the old Irish priest had helped him immensely, in some inexplicable way which he was unable to define. Far from feeling suicidal any more, he had already begun receiving treatment for his addictions and was now actively making plans for his future. Wanting to show his gratitude, he decided to return to the church to thank the priest.

As he was walking down the path towards the door of the presbytery, Dave caught sight of a woman peering through the curtains of the bedroom window. Knowing that she had seen him approaching, he waited at the front door, without knocking, for her to come down the stairs to answer it.

"I'm sorry to bother you," he stammered, suddenly feeling nervous, "but I've come to see the priest."

Before he could say another word, a young priest peered over the woman's shoulder.

"Yes, can I help you" he said.

"No, er, no thankyou," said Dave, apologetically, "I meant the elderly Irish priest."

"I'm the only priest in Saint Hugh's," explained the young man, "I've been here for four years now." Then, turning to the housekeeper, he asked, "you've been here for years, Pat, has there ever been such a priest?" But, before she could answer, he politely made his excuses to leave. "I'm quite sure that Mrs Hague will be able to help you. I'm sorry, I've got to go."

Dave gave the housekeeper a detailed description of the elderly priest and said that he had only surmised that he was from that church. After he had told her the whole story, he offered his apologies and was just about to leave.

"Just a minute," she said, disappearing into the house. A few moments later she reappeared, holding a framed photograph in her hands in such a way as to suggest that it meant a great deal to her.

"Is this the priest you're looking for?" she asked, showing him the photograph.

"Yes," answered Dave, excitedly. "That's him! Where can I find him? Does he still live round here?"

"You'd have a job finding him," she replied. "That's a picture of Father Brendon and he died fifteen years ago."

"Fifteen years ago!" gasped Dave in disbelief, "but I met him in the church and he spoke to me and touched me!"

"It's not the first time that something like this has happened," she went on, smiling nostalgically. "He was such a good man. He was the parish priest in this church for twelve years. I always keep his photograph in my room. It brings back so many happy memories of him. You obviously needed his help."

"Yes," answered Dave, still in a daze. "I certainly did and he did help me."

After thanking Mrs Hague and still feeling totally confused by the whole experience, he turned and walked back down the path towards the gate, pausing for a moment to look back at the church. He could not really believe what he had been told and he was sure that nobody else would believe it either, yet the evidence was there. He had been brought back from the brink of despair by the old priest and, for that, he would be eternally grateful.

"Thank you, Father Brendon," he whispered. "Thank you!"

Lady of the Light

There was once a little boy who was in extremely poor health. He suffered from an acute respiratory disease which was progressive and incurable. His mother prayed constantly for divine intervention to help him get well and she was determined that eventually, despite an extremely bleak prognosis, he would make a full recovery. The doctors did not expect him to survive until his teens and he lived a comparatively sheltered existence, in and out of Alder Hey Children's Hospital. Little wonder then, that he became extremely introverted, with a deep and often touching interest in Christianity. His close relationship with his mother increased his sensitivity and simply made him more and more insecure but his deep faith in God helped him believe that he was not going to die.

Early one dark and cold December night, his friend, Tommy Edgar, was invited round to the house to keep him company. The two friends amused themselves in the parlour, as it was then called, of the terraced house at 30 Grosvenor Road, oblivious to the wind and rain beating fiercely against the window. The room was suddenly plunged into darkness and, almost simultaneously, a light began to shine above an old cabinet that stood against the wall behind the door. Unafraid at first, the two boys peered through the darkness at the strange glow. It gradually took the shape of a lady in long flowing gowns and, as time passed by, the figure became animated and more clearly defined. The two boys were transfixed by the apparition and just stared in disbelief as it grew in brightness and intensity.

"It looks like Our Lady!" said one of them.

"It is her!" declared the other.

Unable to contain his emotion, Tommy Edgar began to cry.

"I want to go home!" he pleaded, groping his way to the parlour door, "I've got to go now."

The commotion caused his Aunt Sadie who had brought him on the visit and the sick boy's mother, to come running in to investigate. The room was still in darkness and the apparition was still apparent over the cabinet behind the door. All four of them stood in awe and disbelief and, when all the possible causes had been eliminated from the equation, they concluded that it was, indeed, an apparition of Our Lady.

The room was left in darkness and the usual prayers to Our Lady were recited. The boy's mother concluded that the apparition had definitely appeared to make her son better. She encouraged him to climb up onto a stool and reach out and touch the phantom lady. However, before his hand was able to make contact with the Lady of Light, the intensity of the glow surrounding her increased once more and then she disappeared completely, leaving the room in darkness. When the lights were switched on again, everyone was filled with a feeling of disappointment and emptiness.

Looking carefully at the surface of the old cabinet, the boy's mother noticed a thin film of pink, iridescent powder. Thinking that it was connected to the apparition and therefore must have some importance, she carefully collected it into an empty tablet bottle, to show to a nun from the local church. The family stayed up late discussing the apparition, trying to decide exactly what it was and what it signified.

On the following day, the mystery deepened when the brown bottle containing the powder was produced to show Sister Margaret, a family friend. All eyes were upon it as the top was carefully removed. However, to everyone's dismay it was found to be completely empty, with no trace left of the evidence! The strange pink powder had vanished!

Local papers put forward their own theories as to what the apparition had been and the Church also made some serious comments about the phenomenon. However, nobody actually ascertained the true significance of the Lady of Light.

Two weeks later, however, disaster struck the family: the little boy developed double pneumonia and his mother also fell seriously ill. In fact, the whole family seemed to be cursed with ill health, with no sign of light at the end of the tunnel. However, against all expectations, their misfortunes came to an abrupt end and it suddenly seemed that there was a much brighter future ahead. The son recovered well from his pneumonia and his mother was also restored to full health and, in a very short while, everything was back to as near normal as possible. In addition, the local church had affirmed that the apparition had truly been of Our Lady, in the role of a mother, coming to reassure another mother that everything would eventually be alright with her child.

Whatever the phenomenon actually was, the little boy is still alive to this day and, what is more, that little boy is me: Billy Roberts!

The Lady of Light appeared to me again in 1975, just before an extremely unfortunate period in my life. Once again, the welcome apparition gave me strength and helped me to face the difficulties which were lying in store for me. Although I no longer have any connections with 30 Grosvenor Road, Wavertree, the house itself is, and always will be, etched upon my heart.

The Ghost of Lawrence Road School

Lawrence Road School was the first that Rob Williams had attended. The year was 1951 and, at the tender age of five, he was taken away from the security of his mother's apron strings and thrown into the clutches of Miss Jones, who was in charge of Class A in the infants school. As it happened, however, Miss Jones was not the ogre whom Rob had thought she would be. On the contrary, she was kind and gentle and could obviously see that little Rob was quite a shy and sensitive child. She immediately took him under her wing and helped him as much as time would allow. He spent an entire two years in Miss Jones' care and became very attached to her and so, when he was seven and had to leave Lawrence Road Infants, to move up to the Junior School, he felt as though his world had been turned upside down. But, like all children, he was very resilient and eventually accepted the move and got on with the rest of his schooling.

The years passed by and Rob Williams finished his education and eventually embarked on his working life. He had no particular career plan and, the age of 20, he found himself between jobs. His father knew Jimmy Rigby, the caretaker in Lawrence Road School, so he was able to put in a good word for him for the position of Junior Porter, which had just become vacant.

Rob managed to get the job and on the morning that he started he felt very nostalgic. To his great surprise, Miss Jones was still teaching in class A and, to his delight, she still remembered him and welcomed him back.

He quickly settled into his new post and every morning, at 8.30 prompt, he could be seen brushing the playground, the first of his daily chores. It was not until the school had broken up for the summer holidays and Rob had been left in charge, that he was made aware of the strange happenings.

It was 4 o'clock in the afternoon and the last two cleaners, Mrs Wilson and Dolly Mullen had shouted goodbye and closed the heavy door behind them. Rob checked the Callow Road entrance after they had gone and could see them walking towards Lawrence Road. He then went back into the school and bolted the door behind him. Jimmy Rigby, the caretaker, was on holiday for two weeks and this was the first time that Rob had been completely alone in the school. His footsteps echoed loudly as he walked along the shadowy empty corridor and he paused for a few moments at the foot of the old stone staircase. A sudden eerie feeling engulfed him and he felt goose bumps erupting all over his skin. He tried to fight against his feeling of uneasiness, because he was responsible for the school and so knew that he had to walk through the deserted corridors to check that all the doors and windows were securely closed.

He began to ascend the stone staircase at the very front of the school, nervously planning the best escape route, should anything untoward happen. He was not usually a nervous person, but being alone in the empty school somehow overwhelmed him and he just wanted the day to be over as quickly as possible.

The doors at the top of the stairs led directly into the corridor of the Junior School and Rob could see quite clearly along this from one end to the other. Although there was nobody there, he could hear footsteps coming from the direction of the back stairs, by the caretaker's room. He was feeling a little afraid, but convinced himself that it was just one of the cleaners whom he had perhaps forgotten about. He did not know all their names yet, but, as far as he could work out, there were about seven in all.

Halfway along the corridor, he felt the presence of someone behind him and turned round quickly to be confronted by a middle-aged man in a dark suit.

"I'm sorry, Ken," said the man. "Did I frighten you?"

"My name is ..." Rob attempted to correct him but the man interrupted him and spoke again.

"I'm looking for Kate," he said, turning his head nervously to look, first down one end of the corridor and then the other.

Rob thought that there was something quite strange about him and eyed him curiously. Kate was obviously one of the cleaners, he surmised, and this person must be her husband. Without saying another word, the man moved quickly down the corridor, in the direction of the back staircase.

"No, you'd better come this way with me!" called Rob. "It's all locked up down that end!"

But the man just ignored him and carried on walking in the same direction.

Rob was alarmed to note that the sound of the man's heavy footsteps on the wooden block floor did not appear to be synchronised with the movement of his feet and he seemed, at times, to be almost gliding across its surface without actually making contact with it. Knowing that the entrance to which the man was obviously heading was locked, he decided to wait until he returned, rather than chase after him.

However, after half an hour had elapsed and the man was still nowhere to be seen, Rob went looking for him but, as far as he could ascertain, the building was completely empty. There was definitely no sign of the strange man.

Despite the strange circumstances, he did not give the incident another thought and simply concluded that the man must have somehow found his own way out of the building. However, the following day, he was chatting to Phoebe, one of the cleaners, over a cup of tea in the boiler room and he just happened to mention the incident with the man. But, before he had a chance to tell her the whole story, she quickly interrupted him.

"He kept calling you Ken?"

"That's right!" said Rob, surprised that she knew. "How did you know that? Do you know him?"

"Erm, not really," and her voice began to fade, "erm, well, sort of..."

"He's a bit of a weird individual," joked Rob, "he's got a funny walk for a start. His feet don't seem to touch the ground!"

"His name is Mr Bridge - Alf Bridge," she continued, sipping her tea and watching

Rob's face for his reaction.

"Is Kate his wife then? Is she one of the cleaners here?"

"There's no one here called Kate," continued Phoebe, in a controlled tone. "Kate's his daughter - er, was his daughter."

"What do you mean, was?" asked Rob, puzzled.

"Kate's dead!" she said sharply, "She was killed during the War ..."

By this time, Rob was completely confused and wanted Phoebe to hurry up and tell him the whole story.

"... and so was Alf Bridge!" She grinned at the shocked look on Rob's face. "They used the hall in the Infants School as a mortuary in the War. Kate is supposed to have been laid in the hall along with her mother and others killed in an air raid. Alf Bridge was divorced from his wife and came in to identify them. He died shortly afterwards from a massive heart attack, but some say he died of a broken heart."

"Blimey!" gasped Rob, "And I spoke to him. Why did he keep calling me Ken?"

"Ken was the caretaker during the War and Alf Bridge knew him."

Rob was dumbfounded and found the whole scenario difficult to believe. He dreaded the very thought of being alone in the school ever again, but he knew that he would probably have to be. That was certainly not the last time that Rob was to come face to face with Alf Bridge.

Many sightings of children were reported at Lawrence Road School through the years. Rob Williams saw the ghost of Alf Bridge on numerous occasions and each time they came face to face he referred to him as Ken.

I have come to the conclusion that the majority of apparitions do not actually see the places they haunt as they are at the present moment but, more often than not, they see them as they were when they were alive. In the case of Alf Bridge, I am quite certain that what Rob Williams saw was not his actual spirit, but a paranormal, photographic impression, trapped somehow on the etheric screen of time. It is my belief that this phenomenon is brought about as a direct consequence of a powerful discharge of emotion, which becomes sealed in time and is occasionally precipitated when contact is made with an incarnate human psyche.

The Man Who was in Two Places at the Same Time

Although extremely rare, the phenomenon of bi-location is the ability to be in two places at the same time. Many people claim to have experienced the phenomenon of astral projection, but these experiences are mostly subjective and can therefore never be properly substantiated. The phenomenon of bi-location, however, is quite objective and so those who are present at the time, can bear witness to the whole phenomenon.

Although there are many such recorded cases, the following episode is one that actually happened in Liverpool in 1890. Edward Dawson lived a very modest life with his wife, Nora, and their two daughters, Isabel and Elaine. Their house was situated in Anfield Road, just around the corner from Sleepers Hill, in the Liverpool 4 area of the city. Edward's family was his whole life and, as a consequence, he had very few friends. He worked as a clerk for a major shipping firm in the city centre and what time he did have for himself, he spent with his two young daughters.

Edward Dawson's secure and happy life began to change drastically when he suddenly lost his job after 12 years of loyal and hard-working service.

"Surplus to requirements!" his boss had said. "Unfortunately, we have to make way for younger men."

Edward was 50 years old and knew that he would find it very difficult to find another job, especially as there was so much unemployment in Liverpool at that time. Like so many middle aged men before him, he found himself on the scrap heap.

The mounting pressures of redundancy and unemployment began to tell on his relationship with his wife, who was only in her mid 30s and quite vivacious. His previously secure marriage began to fall apart and, although it was something which Edward had always tried to prevent, his wife found herself a secretarial position with a firm of solicitors in Dale Street. He became very depressed and used to spend most of his endless hours of free time casually walking through nearby Stanley Park, or just sitting on a bench near the lake, sadly contemplating his whole future. He began to think seriously about ending his life and could see no other course of action open to him. He was quite certain that his wife no longer loved or respected him and thought that his daughters would be better off without him, especially living in an atmosphere of constant arguments and hostility. However, he always managed to postpone the awful deed, just in case something turned up the following day.

As the weeks passed by, the hours his wife worked seemed to become increasingly longer. She frequently arrived home after 8 o'clock at night, offering him a different excuse each time. At first, he did not think anything about it but he then became increasingly suspicious when he caught sight of his wife, just by chance, saying goodbye to a tall, well-dressed gentleman at the corner of the street. Although Edward tried desperately to convince himself that there was absolutely nothing at all in it, his growing insecurities constantly reminded him that she was much younger than he was, as well as being extremely attractive. However, deeming it best not to say anything to Nora, for fear of aggravating the already volatile situation even more, he decided to try and forget about the whole episode. By now, though, his morale was extremely low and, although he tried desperately to put the incident completely out of his mind, the more he struggled to so, the more it came back to haunt him. Finally, he decided that there was only one thing for it, he would have to follow her when she left work each night, if only to put his mind at rest.

His daughters were old enough now to care for themselves and so, each night, for the next three days, Edward carefully followed his wife from work and each time she was accompanied by the same man. On each occasion they went into Rigby's Tavern in Dale Street and stayed there for no longer than 40 minutes. Edward was quite satisfied that there was nothing more to it, but nonetheless decided to follow his wife for a further two days. On the Thursday morning, however, Nora announced that on the Friday night she probably wouldn't be home until late, because of a farewell meal for a work colleague, who was emigrating to America. Edward tried not to show his concern, but was now more determined than ever to find out if she was telling him the truth.

By 5 o'clock on that Friday evening, Edward's deepest fears had been confirmed. He watched Nora leave work with the same man and followed them, as discreetly as he could, to a nearby hotel. She arrived home just before midnight and Edward had already decided not to confront her.

He continued to follow her for the next two weeks and, to his great sadness, her liaison with the man continued. Further enquiries had revealed that the stranger was called James Fairweather, a solicitor at the office where she worked. Edward was consumed with anger and jealousy and could think of nothing other than revenge. Every waking minute he was tormented by the mental image of his wife in the arms of another man. It was the last straw when Nora announced, once again, that she would not be home until late on the following Friday night, this time using the excuse of a backlog of work.

Edward concluded that there was nothing else for it, if she was prepared to destroy his life, then he was most certainly prepared to destroy hers. He retrieved his father's army pistol from the loft, where he had put it after his death five years before. It was still neatly wrapped in its original army issue bag, as clean as the day he had put it in there for safekeeping. He had never fired a gun in his life before and wondered if he would actually be able to do it when the time came. The chamber was full and it was ready to use.

Each day, after taking the children to school, Edward sat at the table with the gun in his hand, mentally replaying his plan over and over again, until he was absolutely certain that he was going to kill them both. By Friday night he was all psyched up and nothing and no one would deter him.

Before making his way into town, he called in at the church in Anfield Road, just to sit quietly for a few minutes and collect his thoughts. He had been recognised by at least three people going into and coming out of the church. There were other people praying silently in the pews and time passed quickly by. He came out of the building feeling no better than when he had gone in, still with a burning anger inside. He walked from Anfield Road to town almost in a dream. In fact, because his mind was so preoccupied with thoughts of vengeance, he could not recall a single part of the journey but seemed to find his way by instinct alone.

He watched his wife leaving work with her lover and trailed them to the same hotel, taking great care not to be seen. He checked his watch nervously, it was 6.30pm. He realised that he had to do the deed quickly, without too much thought, or he may lose his nerve and that would ruin everything. As soon as the pair had checked in at the reception, he pursued them swiftly up the stairs. As they reached the door to their room, he slowly retrieved the pistol from inside his jacket. He could feel himself trembling inside and again wondered if he could really go through with it. As they entered the room, Edward pushed his way inside and, without further thought, shot them both at point blank range, right through the head, one after the other. They slumped to the floor simultaneously, a bright red pool of blood soaking into the thick carpet. Unseen by any witnesses, Edward fled down the corridor, pausing at the top of the stairs to compose himself, before carefully and slowly descending the stairs, one step at a time and managing to leave the hotel looking outwardly calm.

Outside in the fresh evening air, he could still feel his whole body shaking. He couldn't believe what he had just done and wondered what would happen next. The first thing he did was to take a detour to the Pier Head, where he discreetly discarded the pistol into the Mersey. There were many people casually strolling about and he seemed to mingle amongst them unnoticed. The children had been collected from school by a neighbour and so he took his time walking home, trying to come to terms with what he had done. He wondered how the girls would take the awful news but at least now it was over, for Nora, if not for him.

However, by the time that Edward had turned from Sleepers Hill into Anfield Road, he could see that the police were already at his home. He was immediately arrested and taken to the Westminster Road Police Station, where he was charged with the murder of Nora Dawson. By now, though, Edward had become quite proficient at pretending and he insisted that he was innocent. However, the evidence against him was fairly conclusive. It was obvious that his wife had been seeing someone else and it turned out that he had also been seen entering the hotel, even though he had taken every precaution.

On his behalf, requests were put out by his defence counsel for witnesses. More than one person came forward insisting that Edward Dawson was definitely in the church at 6.30pm and also for some time after that; in other words, at exactly the time the murder was committed. The priest also insisted that he had, in fact, spoken very briefly to him at, or around, 6.45pm on that Friday evening. As far as the jury was concerned, he could not possibly have committed the crime and he was immediately acquitted. But there is no doubt about it, Edward Dawson did kill his wife and her lover but this meant that he had to have been in two places at the same time.

A similar case took place in South Wales in the early 1930s. A jealous husband killed both his wife and her lover and was also acquitted on the grounds that he had been seen in two places at the same time.

The Man Who Flew Over Liverpool

This story is one that perhaps is a little difficult to believe and appears to be straight out of the pages of a science fiction novel. I am quite sure that if it took place today, with all the modern technology, it would perhaps be a little more believable. However, the very fact that it took place in the late 18th century makes it even more difficult to accept. Nonetheless, there is recorded evidence that the strange phenomenon was witnessed by six people in Liverpool at the time, all of whom were extremely well-educated, sober and greatly respected in the community of Everton.

Thomas Pyke lived a solitary and modest existence in a little cottage in the Everton area of Liverpool. He was known to be very eccentric and although he had an extremely simple lifestyle, he was believed to be quite wealthy. He was well thought of in the closely knit community and always had a welcoming smile for anyone he met on the street. His close friend, James Bennett, minister of the local church, always tried to encourage him to take a more active part in the community but, as he grew older, he became more and more of a recluse.

Thomas Pyke was a well-educated man with a deep interest in science and, although his close friend was a man of the church, he himself was something of a heretic and was believed to have more than a keen interest in Eastern religions and their philosophical traditions. He had spent the early part of his life in India and had only returned to England to be with his elderly sister who had since died. Walking into the back room of his little cottage was said to be like walking into a mad professor's laboratory. He spent all his time there concocting strange potions and unusual substances.

"It's not good for your health," warned James, afraid that his friend was in danger of losing his mind.

But, although Thomas was in his mid-60s, he had never been ill in his life and looked much younger than his years. James Bennett was frequently amazed by his friend's stamina; he was always up at the crack of dawn and existed on a very frugal diet. This, James was certain, was the reason why he was so fit and full of energy. Three times a day Thomas Pyke would sit quietly in a cross-legged position on the floor of the front room of his cottage. On the odd occasion when James had called on him whilst he was engaged in this unusual practice, he would just shake his head in disbelief and leave quietly without disturbing him.

Thomas was most certainly an unusual man in more ways than one. This was confirmed when he announced to his friend that he would soon be able to fly, just like some of the mystics of the east.

"Fly?" retorted James. "Are you sure you're feeling quite well, Thomas?"

"I've never felt better!" he replied, studying his friend's face for a response. "When I have mastered the technique, I will have to bid you farewell."

"Farewell?" repeated James, with a somewhat wry expression. "Are you planning to leave us, Thomas?"

"It is my intention to fly to India!"

"Fly to India!"

The conversation stopped there. James was convinced that his friend had inhaled the vapour from one of his strange concoctions causing him to lose his mind. He was immediately overwhelmed with concern and, knowing Thomas to be extremely stubborn, wondered how best he could help him.

Thomas could plainly see the concern etched on his friend's face and smiled in appreciation.

"I know all this sounds a little absurd my dear friend," he continued, "but you will see. I promise that you will be the first person to witness my magnificent achievement. You can rest assured, I have certainly not lost my mind!"

James Bennett spent the following few days fretting constantly about his friend and wondered what on earth he could do to help him. He knew that although Thomas Pyke was extremely eccentric, he was also, on another level, intelligent, practical and down to earth. His bizarre announcement about flying was most unusual and out of character and he believed that it was obviously the result of some strange malady which had suddenly befallen him. However, his concern deepened when, throughout the following week, Thomas was nowhere to be found. James had called on him several times each day but he was never at home.

It was a quarter to midnight one late Friday evening and James was writing in his diary, beneath the flickering light of a single oil lamp. There was a fierce storm outside and the beacon on the hill had been lit to guide in-coming sailing ships into the port of Liverpool. The wind and rain were lashing fiercely against the window pane and, as he rose tiredly to his feet to place another log on the fire, there was a loud knock upon his door.

Startled by the late caller, he hesitated briefly, before moving reluctantly towards the door.

"Who's there?" he called out nervously. But his question was only met with silence. "Who is it?" he called again but, once more, there was only silence.

Deciding that it would not be wise to open the door, he turned to walk back towards his desk when he heard his friend calling out to him from the other side of the door.

"It is me, James - Thomas Pyke."

James quickly pulled back the heavy bolts on the door, turned the key and pulled it wide open to let in the stormy night. He could make out the silhouette of his friend standing at the end of the pathway and wondered why he had moved away from the door.

"Come in from the cold, Thomas," he called out to him. "Quickly, come inside before you catch your death!"

"I have done it!" laughed Thomas with a sound of pure joy and pride. "I have actually done it, my dear friend! Watch me!"

James could do nothing but peer curiously through the wind and the rain at his friend. He could see Thomas' coat billowing out in the wind and watched as he held out his arms straight in front of him and threw back his head as though to meet the wind face on.

"Thomas, please come in from the cold!" he pleaded, now convinced that his friend had truly gone mad. "What are you …?"

Before he could finish the sentence, he gasped in amazement, as something seemed to lift Thomas from the ground. He was suspended at least six feet in the air and turned his beaming face towards James standing in the doorway.

"Look, James!" he cried out, his voice echoing on the wind. "I have done it! Watch." And before another word was spoken, Thomas seemed to be propelled upwards into the stormy night until he had disappeared completely from sight. James stood rooted in the doorway, in stunned silence and disbelief. Thomas had vanished!

Although he had witnessed it with his own eyes, James could not believe what he had just seen. He scanned the darkness but Thomas was nowhere in sight. He was completely amazed and eventually closed the door against the darkness and the storm. He sat at his desk in silence, replaying the whole scene slowly in his mind. Then, removing his pen quickly from the ink well, he began to record every detail of the whole incident in his diary, from beginning to end, as if this would help him to make sense of it. At least with a written record, tomorrow he would know that it had not been a dream, or had that he had imagined the whole thing.

The following day the storm had cleared and James lost no time in going round to call upon Thomas. He was greeted eagerly by his friend, who was keen to tell him everything he might want to know about his new ability.

"I have mastered the art of flying," he told him, excitedly. "I have discovered the ancient secret, as taught by the wise men of the east. The secret is in a potion that transforms the mind and makes the body so light that it can travel through the air."

"That is not possible," argued James, trying to stay calm, "only birds can fly."

"But how can you say that?" grinned Thomas. "You saw me fly last night."

"It was an illusion," protested James. "You have mastered the art of illusion, nothing more."

"If that is what you believe," sighed Thomas, "nothing will change your mind until you see me fly again."

Still half believing that he had imagined the whole thing and convinced that Thomas was quite ill, James placed a reassuring hand on his shoulder and tried to appeal to his reason.

"Please, Thomas, allow me to help you."

Thomas shook his head and smiled in disbelief that James had really not believed what he had seen the previous night.

"You really do not believe your own eyes, do you my dear friend?"

James could clearly read the determination in his eyes and now did not know what to believe.

"Please take care, Thomas. Please take care!"

Thomas had made up his mind and just wanted to prove to his friend once and for all that he was not mad and that he had mastered the art of flying. He realised that there was no use in demonstrating his ability to James while he was alone; there had to be other witnesses. The best time to do it, he decided, was when James and the church committee were on their way home from Sunday morning service.

On the following Sunday, totally unaware of what exactly was waiting for them, James Bennett and five members of the church committee casually made their way home from the morning service. It was when they had just reached the stile leading to the brow, that they found themselves suddenly confronted by Thomas Pyke. He stood on the grassy rise just ahead of them, dressed in his winter cape and top hat. He was smiling with excitement and knew full well that his friend was aware of his purpose in being there.

"Thomas!" exclaimed James. "It's good to see you."

The other men looked curiously at each other and wondered why Thomas Pyke had suddenly appeared on top of the rise. They knew him to be quite eccentric and had always been a little wary of him.

"I want you all to bear witness," called Thomas. "I am not as mad as you think, James."

"What on earth is he talking about?" asked one man. "Has he gone completely mad?"

Before anyone else could speak, Thomas took off into the air at an incredible speed. The six men looked on in amazement, until he had disappeared completely from sight. James was spellbound and did not know what to say. They had all seen the strange phenomenon with their own eyes and those who had not seen it would most certainly not believe it.

For several weeks Thomas Pyke had not been seen by anyone and James Bennett was quite convinced that he had been taken away by the devil himself. It was two months later when a letter from overseas arrived at the vicarage. James carefully opened it to discover, with great surprise, that it was from his friend, Thomas Pyke, in India!

He never returned to England, nor did he write again to his good friend, James Bennett. He became part of a legend which somehow got lost in the storyteller's tales and the mists of time …

The Stable that Disappeared

In 1966 Liverpool was alive with the so-called Merseybeat Boom. The mood of the time was captured in the catchphrase, 'love, peace and transcendental meditation', and teenagers came from all over the world to be a part of the Liverpool scene. Phil Kennedy was one such teenager. He was a singer and desperately wanted to be in a Liverpool band. As soon as he had turned 18, he packed his bags, said farewell to his family and made his way from his home in Newcastle, to seek his fame and fortune in Liverpool. He had only £50 in his pocket and one bag containing his clothes. He knew that he could always return home should things not work out for him, but he had already made a contact at a musical festival in London three months previously and so he was certain that Liverpool was the place to be.

He had arranged to meet a friend at 7pm at a pub in the city centre, from where he was to be taken to a flat in Toxteth. By 9.30pm that evening, Phil was on to his fourth drink and his contact had still not arrived. Luckily, he had a phone number to call, should anything go wrong but, when he tried it, he found to his disappointment, that the line was discontinued. By this time it was after 10pm and he was becoming concerned and beginning to feel extremely tired after his journey. He needed somewhere to crash for the night.

Throwing his bag over his shoulder, he began to make his way out of the city centre in search of a cheap hotel or boarding house. As he was so tired, he decided to get on a bus outside the Adelphi Hotel. It was quite crowded with young people who seemed to be heading for a concert being held on a farm the following day on the outskirts of Liverpool. A guy with long hair and a beard spoke to Phil and asked if he, too, was going to the concert. Phil told the stranger the whole story and he was very sympathetic.

"I work with horses on a farm," he told him, eagerly. "It's near where the concert is being held. I live in a disused stable that my boss is renovating. You're welcome to stay for a few days if you like."

Phil was delighted and immediately accepted the stranger's offer. The prospect of having to return home to a great deal of ridicule did not appeal to him. He only needed somewhere to crash for a couple of nights and then he was sure he would find something more permanent.

"That's great," said Phil, gratefully. "A couple of nights should do it! By the way, my name's Phil," and he shook the stranger's hand.

"My name's Clay," the stranger said. "You'll have to take me as you find me. It's an old stable and nothing fancy."

"That's fine by me. I've stayed in far worse places back in Newcastle. Anyway, I'm so tired, I'll just be happy to get my head down."

The stranger had not in any way exaggerated his position, the stable was just a stable and in an extreme state of chaos. They found their way by the light of a single oil lamp, which Clay lit as soon as they entered the wooden building. There was a carpet of straw, a table and a chair, a blanket and a sleeping bag.

"You take the sleeping bag," offered Clay, generously. "I'll be OK with the blanket."

Phil's host made him a cup of tea and they sat and chatted for over an hour.

"By the way," said Clay, "I should tell you that the stable is haunted!"

"Haunted?" grinned Phil with disbelief. "What by?"

"The place is ancient," continued Clay. "It's over a hundred years old. Eighty years ago William Buxton owned it. In fact, he owned the farm as well and quite a lot of land in the area. His favourite horse was stabled here. He came home drunk one night to find that the horse had got out and had strayed into a nearby field. When he finally caught it, he was so furious that he beat it to death with a chain. The stable lad tried to intervene and William Buxton killed him also."

The stable was divided into two parts and the part where Phil and his host were to sleep had been separated from the section where the horse had been killed by a wooden partition. Clay explained to Phil that he would probably be woken up by the sound of clanging chains and horses' hooves clattering on the cobbles.

"The most horrific sound comes later on," warned Clay, looking quite unsettled. "That's the sound of the stable lad pleading for his life." He was silent for a few moments before he spoke again. "But he is not always heard."

Phil was a sceptic where such things were concerned, but tried not to appear too discourteous to his host. In fact, he did not expect to hear anything once his eyes were closed. He was so tired and was aching to go to sleep. He made his excuses and, within moments, he was fast asleep.

It was about 1am when something abruptly disturbed Phil's sleep, causing him to sit bolt upright, wide awake.

He could see that Clay was not there and thought that he had probably gone to the toilet. He concluded that he must have been woken up by Clay's movements and waited for his return, before attempting to go back to sleep. The oil lamp was still lit and sent jerky shadows flickering across the stable floor. The effect was quite eerie and he began to feel more than a little unsettled.

He heard a door open with a loud creak in the adjacent part of the stable and expected Clay to come back in at any moment. The sound of the creaking door was heard twice and was immediately followed by neighing accompanied by the clanging of chains and the rattle of horses' hooves moving across the floor. This cacophony continued for at least 15 minutes, just as Clay had predicted and still there was no sign of him returning. Phil was, by this point, feeling quite afraid and seriously considered leaving. In order to do that, however, he would have to pass through the part of the stable where all the commotion was taking place. He decided that his only option was to stay put and just hoped that the ghostly sounds would come to an end soon.

Eventually silence descended upon the stable once more and all that could be heard was the even thump of Phil's heart as it beat against his ribs. He was so relieved and was just about to settle down again, when the chain began to clang once more, followed by the most unmerciful screams. This lasted for a further two minutes, then everything fell silent once again. The whole spooky scenario left him feeling so drained and exhausted that he was unable to keep his eyes open any longer and he fell into a heavy, troubled sleep.

The following morning the sun shone brightly through the grimy, cobwebbed stable window and Phil had already decided that he would definitely not be staying on for another night, no matter how limited his other options. He could see Clay sleeping and he took the opportunity to beat a silent and hasty retreat.

Deciding to swallow his pride and return home to the security of his family, he caught the next available train back to Newcastle. Some weeks later, however, his mother and father decided to take a trip to Liverpool with Phil and his sister Claire. On his suggestion, the family agreed to visit the stable on the outskirts of Liverpool, so that he could see where the ghostly happening had actually taken place. To his surprise, in the spot where he was sure that the stable had been, there now stood a huge block of flats.

"Are you quite certain it was here?" enquired his mother, somewhat sceptical about the whole story. "You're probably mistaken!"

"No, it was definitely here," he insisted. "I remember those houses across the road and that petrol station on the corner."

He was totally confused about the whole affair but he was equally determined to prove to his parents that it actually did happen and that the stable had been there just as he had described it. He had noticed a library further along the road and asked his father to drive him there. The elderly librarian listened with interest to Phil's fascinating story, before reaching under the counter to retrieve a large green file. She opened it, somewhere in the middle and turned it round for Phil to read. It told the story of the haunted stable that had been burned to the ground in 1904, when it was decided that no good would ever come of it. The file confirmed the story which Phil had been told by his host at the stable and went on to say:

'Clay Morris, the 25-year-old stable lad, tried to intervene and stop William Buxton from beating the horse to death, but he himself was murdered. The ghosts of the horse and Clay Morris still cry out in anguish and desperation …'

Phil could not believe what he was reading. Not only was the stable he had stayed in destroyed in 1904 by fire, but also, the lad who had taken him there in the first place was actually a ghost - the ghost of Clay Morris …

Although opinions vary greatly as to the exact whereabouts of the stable, it is thought to have been somewhere around the area of Chiselhurst Avenue in Belle Vale, where there is now a large housing development of houses and flats.

A Father's Love Knows No Bounds

Annie Walker's husband, Jack, had been killed in the First World War and now she was faced with the sad prospect of bringing up four young children alone. Together they lived in Nesfield Street, off Sleeper's Hill in Anfield, in a little two-up and two-down terrace. Jack had been a good father and had always provided for his family and, although Annie was a strong woman, she now found herself in a desperate situation, with rent to pay and children to clothe and feed.

Knowing of her plight, a friend told her about a vacancy in the Bronte pub nearby and, by the weekend, she found herself in the position of barmaid. She did not particularly enjoy the job, but at least it was work and helped her to provide for her family.

Annie Walker was an attractive woman and it was not long before she caught the attention of a handsome young man by the name of Billy Eden. The couple fell in love and within a short space of time they were married. Although conditions were quite cramped in their small terraced house, they lived together reasonably happily as a family and Billy Eden willingly took on the role of father to Annie's four small children.

The first sign of trouble came when Annie had her first child to Billy. His attitude to his stepchildren gradually began to change and when she gave birth to his second child, his feelings towards them altered completely. He became cruel and hostile and sometimes quite violent towards them. He took pains to show them that his own children were far more important to him and that he did not really care for them at all. He would frequently make them wait for their meals until his own children had finished theirs.

Over the years, the situation gradually deteriorated and he began to take his aggression and hatred out on his youngest stepdaughter, Annie. Because she was quite defiant towards him, he vented his anger even more vehemently against her and would beat her for the most insignificant of reasons. It was much worse when he was drunk, as he often was, particularly when his work as a bricklayer had temporarily stopped, perhaps because of bad weather. Annie Walker's two older sons could not wait to leave home to get away from their stepfather but, in the meantime, they had to put up with his drunken aggression.

It all changed one winter's evening, two weeks before Christmas, when young Annie was helping her mother to prepare the evening meal. She was singing cheerfully in the kitchen, content in the fact that she was helping her mother, when she heard the key turn in the front door. The merriment abruptly stopped and the atmosphere changed completely as Billy Eden came into the kitchen, swaying drunkenly from side to side and cursing under his breath. Young Annie could feel her heart beating hard against her ribs as he came up close to her. She could smell the alcohol on his breath and waited for the sudden eruption of his temper, as was always the case when he came home in that state. Even his own children had begun to show some fear of him and were now sitting quietly in the living room.

He swore at young Annie and she moved carefully away from him. This annoyed him and he hit her sharply across the face, the force of the blow knocking her to the ground. He went to grab her as she rose to her feet, but she pushed him away and made her way towards the stairs. Enraged, Billy Eden drunkenly undid his broad leather belt and slid it off.

"I'll teach you!" he yelled menacingly, as he pursued her up the stairs.

Annie was halfway up when she felt his enormous sweaty hand grab hold of her leg and she screamed as he began lashing her viciously with the belt, intent on doing her serious damage, his uncontrollable blind rage burning like fire in his eyes.

All at once, a man's voice was heard coming from the top of the stairs.

"No! Stop!" the voice commanded loudly.

Billy Eden loosened his grip on his terrified young victim as his eyes moved to the top of the stairs. He was confronted by the figure of a tall man towering above him on the landing, who was pointing his finger accusingly at him. The man then closed his hand into a fist and shook it menacingly at Billy Eden, causing him to fall backwards to the bottom of the stairs where he lay, unconscious, for a couple of minutes. Annie could not believe what she had just seen and she ran to tell her mother all about it.

"It was Daddy," she sobbed. "He saved me!"

The child was far too young to remember her father in person, but she recognised him from some photographs that her mother had kept of him, for the children's sake. He had returned from the grave to protect his daughter and to show her that love transcends time and death. Not surprisingly, the whole episode was a great shock to Billy Eden and he changed from that day onwards and was never violent to his stepchildren again.

My mother, whose maiden name was Annie Walker, told me this story.

Kitty Stone and the Haunted Tree

Even the most sceptical person has to admit to being more than a little curious about the supernatural. There is a certain element in all of us which enjoys being afraid, within limits, and whether or not we care to admit it, most of us are fascinated by those things in life which we do not fully understand. I am of the firm belief that the phenomenon of the mind is not peculiar to the human species alone, but that every part of the so-called inanimate world around us also has a mind of sorts and is capable of storing memories. The older the object, the more comprehensive and longer the memories held within its mass. This story is about an ancient oak tree in a Liverpool park, believed to be over one thousand years old. Under the shade of this tree, hundreds of years ago, it is believed that trials once took place. Although the tree now stands as a pitiful shell, its branches needing artificial support, it was once a fine, strong and healthy oak. Many legends surround the ancient oak tree in Calderstones Park, but the tree alone knows the whole truth.

In 1647, Kitty Stone was known affectionately by the locals as the 'lady with the seeing eye'. She was a most unusual woman, with many strange powers, who was often called upon by those in need of her healing touch. Those who consulted her believed that she could see right into their souls and would therefore be able to detect exactly what was wrong with them. Once she had made her diagnosis, she would either endeavour to heal them with a touch of her hand, or prescribe a vile-tasting infusion of herbs and berries, to be taken in equal portions over the period of one month.

Kitty lived alone in a little cottage in nearby Gateacre, with only her black cat, Sam, for company. Quite often, those who consulted her did so anonymously and would often deny all knowledge of the old woman, if questioned. For many, it was much better to keep it that way, as the church did not take kindly to such people as Kitty Stone. She had already attracted the attention of the local clergy, who were now keeping a watchful eye on her activities and some church people had already tried to incite the village folk to turn against her. Although there were many who respected and cared greatly for Kitty, there were few who would actually declare their friendship publicly, for fear that they, too, would eventually be brought under the scrutiny of the church, which was very powerful in those days. Her friends knew that it was just a matter of time before she would be publicly branded a heretic, the consequence of which could mean only one thing - death!

Despite being fully aware of all this, Kitty was not afraid and refused to change anything about her life, or curtail her activities, regardless of the possible consequences to herself.

James Ashcroft was a soldier, who had just returned from the South of England to find his wife very ill with a high fever. Although the physician had been called, his prognosis was bleak.

"She will die!" he informed the young soldier, bluntly. "There is nothing I can do for her!"

James Ashcroft was quite determined that Jessica, his wife of only six months, was not going to die and, although he was a religious man, he called at Kitty Stone's little cottage late that night and pleaded with her to come and attend to his young wife.

"I don't want to lose her," he cried, the anguish he was suffering clearly written clearly on his handsome young face. "Please help her."

Kitty took her time collecting all the things she needed. Then, placing her woollen shawl carefully about her shoulders, she followed James to his home. His young wife was still burning with fever and had by now lapsed into a deep sleep, or coma. Kitty stared at her for a few moments, then declared in a low voice, "She'll be fine!" She turned to the young soldier and instructed him to leave her alone with his wife for a short while and reluctantly he left the room.

No more than five minutes had elapsed when Kitty called him back inside. He was shocked but delighted to find his wife sitting bolt upright in bed and she appeared bright-eyed with colour in her cheeks once again.

"Jessica," he exclaimed, in disbelief, kissing her forehead. "My dear, you are well!"

Kitty smiled to herself and left the room, quietly and unobtrusively, unnoticed by the couple, who were oblivious to anything but each other.

James Ashcroft was so excited that his wife had seemingly made a full and remarkable recovery, despite the physician having declared so emphatically that she was going to die, that he announced it at the church service on the following Sunday morning. This angered both the physician and the minister, who both denounced her as an evil force.

"Something must be done about that wicked woman," demanded the physician, furiously. "She has deliberately tried to undermine me. If nothing is done about her soon, I will lose my credibility and respect as the village physician."

The minister agreed wholeheartedly, as his position was similarly affected and he immediately called a meeting of the church committee. They took only 15 minutes to reach their conclusion, which was that, "Kitty Stone is a witch and must be dealt with accordingly."

The local magistrate was consulted and a warrant for her arrest was issued. She was brought before the magistrate and the church committee, who had together assembled secretly beneath the old oak tree. There was no one to speak in Kitty's favour and the whole process was over within 20 minutes.

"We must make an example of this wretched woman," insisted the physician. "We simply cannot allow this sort of practice to take place."

"I totally agree," added the magistrate, "but we must first allow her to speak in her own defence."

He turned to Kitty and asked her if she had anything to say. She smiled and shook her head.

"You cannot find me guilty of anything," she said, calmly. "What have I done that is so wrong?"

"You are a heretic," stated the magistrate, as a matter of fact. "You defile the name of God by your actions."

"What I do, I do in the name of God," she affirmed. "What wrong is there in that?"

"You see!" interjected the physician. "She claims to do the work of God. She is a practitioner of the black arts. She is a witch, she must die!"

Suddenly, a lone voice called out, "No!" from the back of the small crowd which had gathered to watch the proceedings and James Ashcroft stepped forward to address the assembly.

"She is a good woman. She saved my wife from death when the physician himself said she was going to die."

"I say that this man is in league with the old witch," replied the physician, defensively, pointing an accusing finger at the young soldier.

"If he is in league with her, then so must his wife also be in league with her," the magistrate concluded, switching his attention to the young soldier.

"They must all die," pronounced the minister, raising his fist in anger. "We must destroy them, before they destroy us!"

The angry mood quickly spread throughout the crowd and the magistrate proclaimed the three of them guilty and ordered them to be hanged. The young soldier and Kitty Stone were bound tightly together and, with no further questions asked, the two were taken over to the strongest and straightest branch of the old oak tree. They were forced to stand beneath it until James Ashcroft's wife had been brought to join them.

"Save yourself," urged the magistrate. "Admit that you are in league with the witch and we will spare both you and your wife."

James Ashcroft refused to betray Kitty Stone, but begged for his wife to be spared. But the magistrate ignored his pleas.

"There is nothing more to be said," he concluded solemnly. "Hang them!"

Within moments, a noose was placed firmly around each of their necks, followed by a few prayerful utterances from the minister. Kitty Stone cursed each of her persecutors in turn, by name, and then murmured a fateful prophecy.

"The oak tree from where we hang, shall, for many years, bear witness to this day."

The magistrate nodded his head and, within moments, the three accused were suspended four feet from the ground. A shocked silence descended on the crowd until the last breath was heard. As Kitty Stone breathed her last, her black cat, Sam, was seen to encircle the oak tree three times, before curling up to die beneath its mistress. This, it was said, was confirmation that Kitty Stone was indeed a witch, 'and their spirits together the old oak embraced …'

The ancient oak still stands in Calderstones Park, a silent witness to what was thought to have been an illegal hanging, so many years ago. It is said that if you stand quietly, as close to the tree as possible, Kitty Stone's curse can still be heard. Many claim to have seen Kitty and her black cat taking a leisurely stroll by the old tree, then suddenly disappearing into nothingness. If you approach the tree at dusk, it is said that you can see the actual hanging taking place, almost like a video replaying the images from the past.

The Heart on the Window

Rodney Street is perhaps the ideal setting for a Victorian drama and it is most certainly a street with a great deal of atmosphere and character. In fact, the whole area is steeped in history, with innumerable tales of ghosts and phantoms roaming the once gaslit street in the dead of night. Looking at the tall Victorian buildings, it is not difficult to allow one's imagination to be transported back through time, to that period when elegant, bonneted ladies, escorted by men dressed in top hats and capes, were quite a commonplace sight. Although tarmac has now replaced the cobbles across the streets, it is claimed that horse drawn handsome cabs can still be heard, in the hush of night, as they make their way home down Rodney Street, through the memories of time.

In 1898, Nellie Broadhurst was 18 years old and lived with her mother, father and two younger sisters, Emma and Sarah, at 24 Rodney Street, across the road from St Andrew's Church. Nellie's father, Charles Broadhurst, ran his own business in the Liverpool city centre, but spent most of his time commuting to and from London. Her mother, Margaret, was a lady of leisure, but involved herself as much as she possibly could in a local charity for the poor. It was because of that charity that Nellie's life changed completely when she was introduced to 28-year-old Edward Dunbar for the first time, one December evening just before Christmas.

She had been preparing her gown for the Masonic Ball, to be held on Boxing Night, and was awaiting the arrival of her mother, who had gone into the city centre to do some shopping. Nellie's two sisters were playing upstairs and she was sitting in front of the fire in the drawing room, intently altering the hem of her new dress, when her concentration was suddenly broken by the sound of the front door closing. Nellie rushed into the hall to greet her mother, only to discover that a tall, well-dressed young man had accompanied her into the house. Before Nellie could speak, her mother introduced him.

"Nellie, this is Edward Dunbar, he has just moved to Liverpool and is in charge of the charity's finances."

"Hello," said Nellie, shyly, "I'm pleased to meet you."

It was quite obvious to Nellie's mother that her daughter was immediately taken with the handsome young Edward Dunbar and Nellie herself could feel her cheeks suddenly flush, as he took her hand.

"Not as much as I am to meet you," he added politely.

For a brief moment Nellie's mother felt an uncomfortable silence, with her daughter being totally mesmerised by Edward's deep blue eyes.

However, Nellie was brought quickly down to reality when her two young sisters entered the room, squabbling about a doll and pulling and shoving each other.

"And who are these two pretty young things?" Edward joked. "I can see that beauty runs in the family."

His gaze strayed once more over to Nellie and she lowered her eyes with embarrassment.

"You will stay for some tea, won't you Edward?" Nellie's mother interjected awkwardly. "Charles is due home shortly, he'd love to meet you."

"I would have loved to," he said, "but I'm afraid I have to meet my brother in Bootle at eight o'clock."

Later on, over the evening meal, Nellie could speak about nothing else but Edward Dunbar and the very next day he made an excuse to call again.

Over the weeks that followed, he saw quite a lot of young Nellie and, with the permission of her parents, on Sundays he would take her for long walks in the park. It was quite clear to Margaret and Charles Broadhurst that the young couple were now very much in love and so it came as no surprise when Edward asked Nellie's father for her hand in marriage. Although they had known each other for a very short time, both her parents agreed that their marriage would be a wonderful thing.

It was a bright and clear spring afternoon, and Edward had presented Nellie with a beautiful diamond engagement ring. He slipped it onto her finger in the presence of both her parents and her young sisters and then announced that he had promised to accompany his brother on an important business trip to France, but assured Nellie that he would be gone for no longer than three weeks. He also promised her that they would marry on his return.

Four weeks passed by and Edward had still not returned as he had promised. Nellie missed him terribly and wondered how she could survive another week without him. He had been gone nearly six weeks when Margaret Broadhurst brought home some very sad news.

"My dear," she began, in a low, serious voice, "I'm afraid I have some very bad news for you." She gestured for Nellie to sit down next to her on the settee. "I am afraid that your beloved Edward has been killed in France! He was knocked over by a runaway horse."

Her words numbed Nellie's brain and for a moment she was unable to speak.

"No! It can't be true!" she uttered weakly. "He promised he would return. We are to be married!"

After the news had finally sunk in, Nellie fell into a decline and would not speak to anyone. For weeks she refused to leave her room at the top of the house and just sat at the window staring down into Rodney Street, still half hoping that it had all been a terrible mistake and that she would soon see Edward knocking at her door, just as he had promised.

Nellie used her engagement ring to scratch Edward's name onto the glass of the picture frame window in her room. She encircled it with a heart and would touch it gently with her fingertips each day, as the tears trickled down her pale cheeks. Her parents tried desperately to encourage her to get on with her life, but she refused and instead sank further into depression.

On the 6 April, exactly 12 months after Edward had been killed, Nellie Broadhurst passed away in her sleep. The post-mortem revealed her to be quite healthy and no physical cause for her death could be found. The family doctor therefore concluded that she had probably died of a broken heart. Her mother and father were devastated but knew now that their daughter was happy and was reunited with the man she had loved and been with for so short a time.

One afternoon, Margaret Broadhurst was clearing out some things from Nellie's room and she sat for a moment reminiscing and sadly watching the sun casting shapes onto the wall, just as Nellie had done as a child. The heart which she had lovingly scratched with her ring on the window caught Margaret's attention and curiosity led her to take a closer look. She knew that Nellie had scratched Edward's name inside the heart but, to her surprise, she could see that Nellie's name was now there also, but had obviously been scratched in by a different hand. Margaret knew for certain that it was not her husband's writing and the two girls were far too young to have done such a thing. A cold shiver suddenly went through her body, as she compared the writing on the window with Edward's writing on the card that he had sent to Nellie at Christmas. It was exactly the same, even though she knew it must have been scratched on the window sometime after Edward himself had died. The date beside the heart confirmed when it had been done, the 9th April, three days after Nellie had died.

Although she is now with her beloved Edward, Nellie Broadhurst is often seen sitting staring sadly through the window on the top floor of 24 Rodney Street. People in the house have said that they have seen young Nellie sitting quietly by the window and that she only disappears when there has been some movement in the room. Witnesses have also noticed that her appearance is quite often accompanied by an overwhelming smell of flowers.

I am quite certain that what is seen at 24 Rodney Street is not actually the spirit of Nellie Broadhurst, but an emotional image of her, trapped in the subtle atmosphere of the house itself. Such emotion has been discharged into the psychic structure of the house and images of events are constantly replayed, rather like watching an old movie over and over again. Eventually the emotional energy will burn itself out and disappear forever.

The Man Who Received a Phone Call from Himself

Ken Monroe was 51 years old and everyone said that he was a prime candidate for a heart attack. He had an extremely demanding job with a publisher, which involved travelling extensively all over the world. He was very rarely home these days and yet he seemed to thrive on the stress which his work created. His wife, Monica, was always pleading with him to take it easy, even trying to persuade him to take early retirement. The very thought of retiring made Ken laugh out loud. He had to work and apart from his family, his work was his life. Thanks to Ken's hard work and determination, the Monroes were now quite comfortably off. Their detached house overlooked Calderstones Park, in what was considered to be one of the nicer and more refined parts of Liverpool. They each had a car and their 10-year-old twin daughters were now at a prestigious private school in Sefton Park.

Ken had always wanted to move away from Liverpool and had only stayed in the city for Monica's sake. She had promised him that she would move as soon as the children were older and so, until then, his dream of an Elizabethan cottage in Kent would have to wait.

As a realist, Ken was extremely practical and down to earth. He was not a tactile person and only ever showed his emotions on rare occasions, perhaps when he had had a little too much to drink, as was always the case at Christmas. His family meant everything to him and, as far as he was concerned, all that he did, was for their sake. It never occurred to him that his wife might be right when she kept on telling him to take it easy.

"More men die of heart attacks at your age than at any other," she had warned him. "You should take it easy at your time of life. Think of me and the girls, if you won't think of yourself."

"I don't know why you go on about it so much," he argued. "I'm as fit as fiddle."

Although Ken worked away most weekends, he had arranged to stay at home on one particular Sunday, to be with his wife and daughters.

"I'll book a table at a restaurant in town," he suggested, "and then we'll take a drive out to Wales, perhaps we could even take a picnic. We haven't done that for ages and the kids would love it."

Monica was delighted and could not wait to tell the girls when they arrived home from school that afternoon. This would be the first Sunday they had spent together as a family in ages. However, on the Friday night, Ken received an e-mail from his boss, informing him that it had been arranged for him to travel on Sunday morning to their branch in Zurich. Naturally, Monica was furious, this was a scenario with which she was only too familiar.

"What will I tell the girls?" she snapped. "They're so excited. You really are awful, you know, Ken. You just can't say no to your boss, can you?"

"It's work, you know that! It's what I do. What choice have I got? It pays the bills and allows us to keep the lifestyle we have."

"Some lifestyle when we can't even have a day out together!"

At this, Monica stormed angrily from the room, slamming the door behind her. Ken sat quietly for a moment, feeling a little guilty. He tried to contact his boss on the telephone, hoping to persuade him to get somebody else to make the trip, but the boss's wife told Ken that he had already gone to London on business. There was nothing else for it, Ken knew that he had to go to Zurich now, but he would make it up to his wife and daughters on his return. He was beginning to realise the effect that his work was actually having on his family and he was determined to make some changes in the near future.

The following morning he was driving along Dale Street when his mobile phone rang. He turned down Stanley Street and pulled over to the side of the road to take the call.

"Hello," he said, half expecting it to be his wife, but there was only silence on the other end of the line. "Hello," he said again, "who's speaking?"

"Hello," came the reply, "who's speaking?"

The response on the other end of the phone came almost simultaneously with the sound of his own voice and so Ken realised that it was just an echo that he could hear, nothing more.

"These wretched mobile phones," he cursed, throwing it onto the passenger seat, where it rang again almost immediately and for a moment he ignored it, thinking that it would soon stop. But the phone kept on ringing and Ken answered it. "Hello!" shouted impatiently.

"Hello," answered the voice.

"Who's speaking?"

"Who do you think it is?" the voice retorted, sarcastically. "It's you, who else?"

At first, Ken thought it was somebody playing a joke on him and he was just about to turn the phone off, when the voice spoke again.

"I wouldn't turn it off if I were you."

Ken was silent for a few moments, wondering how the person on the other end of the phone knew that he was going to turn off his mobile.

"Hello," Ken said, breaking the silence. "Are you still there?"

"Of course I'm still here," the voice retorted sharply. "You're still there, aren't you?"

"Yes ..." Ken stuttered nervously. "Who is this speaking?"

"I've told you - it's you, who else?"

"This is bloody ridiculous," snapped Ken. "Whoever you are, what in God's name do you want?"

"I don't want to die," said the voice. "Don't go on that trip to Zurich. The plane is going to crash!"

Ken felt a cold shiver pass through his body. If it was somebody playing a joke on him, it was a very sick joke he thought to himself.

"What do you mean?" he stammered clumsily. "You don't want to die - plane crash? Are you travelling on the plane?"

"Of course I'm travelling on the plane," replied the voice. "I am totally at your mercy. My fate is completely in your hands."

"What do you mean?"

"I've already told you," the voice continued, as if exasperated by having to repeat the obvious, "you are speaking to yourself."

"This is bloody ridiculous," snapped Ken, angrily. "Who the hell are you? What kind of a stupid game are you playing?"

"Believe me," laughed the voice. "This is no game, I only wish it was. I thought you would at least listen to yourself, but our wife is right, you're as stubborn as a mule. Anyway, don't say I haven't warned you!"

The telephone suddenly went dead and Ken immediately turned it off. He sat in the car for a few minutes, replaying the whole strange incident over in his mind. Deciding it was somebody playing a trick on him, he considered it best not to mention it to Monica.

Although he tried desperately to put it all from his mind, it bothered him terribly and kept breaking into his thoughts. He spent the whole afternoon half-heartedly doing his job and even when he was talking to clients, his mind was still on the strange call. At five o'clock prompt, his mobile rang again. He was in the middle of a conversation with one of his business associates at the time and so he answered it almost absent-mindedly.

"Hello," he said, only half listening for the reply.

"Have you decided yet?" said the voice. "About the Zurich trip."

Ken went cold and felt his heart skip a beat.

"Who is that?"

"Oh, for goodness sake! Don't start that nonsense again," answered the voice, impatiently. "It's you - you know quite well who it is."

Ken asked his business associate to excuse him for a moment whilst he went into the adjacent room to take the call.

"Look here, what's going on? Who the hell are you?"

"This is ridiculous," answered the voice. "We've been through all this before. I'm the only one you will listen to because you are selfish, arrogant and self-opinionated. You might want to die, but I certainly do not and if you don't cancel the trip to Zurich, we will both die."

The phone went dead and Ken just stood there, ashen faced and silent.

"Are you alright, Ken?" asked his friend peering round the door. "You look awful."

"I'm fine," he said, forcing a smile to his lips. "I'm OK, honestly."

Ken had to admit to himself that it did sound like his voice at the other end of the phone. Whether it was someone playing a joke on him, or not, he was anxious and afraid and did not want to go to Zurich. By 8 o'clock that night, Ken had more or less made up his mind. He could not take that trip. He had worried about it so much that now he really did feel quite sick. Monica had noticed that he was quiet and tried to

49

encourage him to talk about whatever it was that was worrying him. He knew that he could not tell his wife, she would think that he had finally lost his mind.

"Right!" said Ken, breaking his silence at last. "That's it, I'm not going to Zurich!"

Monica looked puzzled and wondered why he had reached such a sudden and spontaneous decision.

"That's wonderful, dear!" she smiled vaguely, thinking that he was just being sulky and that he would probably go anyway.

"No, I mean it," he grinned, jumping to his feet. "I'm going to leave a message with the boss's wife. I'll say that I've come down with some sort of tummy bug." And he left the room to use the telephone in the hall.

On Sunday morning Ken was up bright and early. After breakfast he appeared quite restless and kept checking the time on the clock in the corner of the room. By 11 o'clock he was thinking that he would be on the plane, probably ordering his first gin and tonic. He sat back in his armchair and tried to relax. It was no use worrying about it now, he assured himself, the plane would be taking off any minute.

He decided to put the whole thing completely from his mind and to make the most of the weekend with his family. In a cheerful mood, he went ahead and booked a table at a restaurant, as originally planned and then announced that they would all be staying at a hotel in Wales for the night. Then came the grim news flash on the television. The plane to Zurich had crashed, leaving no survivors.

Ken could not believe what he was hearing. He went numb from head to foot and was unable to speak for quite some time. His mind could not comprehend the awfulness of what had happened and of how he had managed to cheat death by not getting on the plane. He thought about the telephone call and the strange conversation with the voice which had claimed to be him. Whatever, or whoever it was, they had undoubtedly saved his life and for that he would always be thankful.

The Mysterious Caller

Brenda Gibson had lived in Newhouse Road, Wavertree for eight years and had decided that it was now time to make a few changes to her life. She had been divorced for two years and although her ex-husband, Ron, still called to see the children and had often intimated that he would very much like to be involved with her again, she had no plans of ever returning to him.

"Never go back!" her mother had always advised as a general matter of principle. "Always look forward."

And that was exactly what Brenda intended to do.

She had been to the estate agents in Allerton Road to find out what sort of prices the houses were fetching in the area, and had immediately taken the decision to sell up and move to Southport, where she had always wanted to live. Now that she was in a much better financial situation, she just knew that the time was right for her to make a new start.

On the Friday afternoon, after the children had gone back to school, Brenda had decided to catch the bus into town to treat herself to a new coat and shoes. She was just about to leave the house, when the telephone rang. The caller asked to speak to someone called Jean and when she told him that he must have the wrong number, he became abusive and then hung up. Although the call had unnerved her somewhat, she quickly put it from her mind and made her way towards Picton Road to catch the bus into town.

On her return, she had no sooner put the key in the lock, than she heard the telephone ringing again. She deposited her shopping on the floor in hallway and quickly rushed to answer it.

"Where have you been?" demanded the voice at the other end of the line. "I've been trying to get you all afternoon."

It was the same man who had been so abusive earlier and Brenda felt a rush of fear, which caused her heart to beat faster.

"Who is this?" she asked, desperately trying not to appear afraid. "I have told you, no one called Jean lives here. If you ring again, I'll have to call the police."

The man became abusive once more and even addressed her by her name. He also appeared to know that she was divorced and that she lived alone with her daughters. Brenda quickly hung up on him. She could feel herself shaking and did not know what to do next. As she stood by the telephone, trying to decide whether or not to call the police, it began to ring again. She allowed it to keep on ringing for some time without answering it, but the persistent noise eventually prompted her to pick up the receiver. At first she did not speak and simply listened. She could hear someone breathing at the other end of the line and some of her fear was replaced by a sudden rush of anger.

"I've just phoned the police!" she shouted down the phone, half expecting him to hang up.

"No you haven't!" he replied, with an arrogant, sneering tone to his voice. "You haven't phoned anyone. You'd better take care, living alone with your two lovely little daughters!"

"You're a pervert!" She screamed, slamming the phone down.

The telephone call had left her feeling emotionally drained and she decided, almost immediately, to carry out her threat and call the police.

It took the police some time to respond to her complaint, but eventually a policewoman called at the house to investigate, the following afternoon. Although she took down all the details of the anonymous calls, Brenda noticed that she seemed completely uninterested in the incidents and appeared to be only half taking notice of what she was saying. So she expressed her deep concern and stressed that she desperately wanted something to be done about it.

The abusive telephone calls came every day at the same time and, on each occasion, Brenda reported them to the police without any satisfaction. Eventually, she called into Lawrence Road Police Station to lodge a formal complaint. She filled in a statement there and then and was assured that something would be done and she had no sooner returned home, than the duty sergeant at the police station rang her.

"We are putting a trace on all your calls," he reassured her. "There's no guarantee that we'll catch the caller, but at least it might deter him."

Satisfied that the police were now going to do something about the problem, Brenda breathed a sigh of relief and sat down with a nice cup of tea and a digestive biscuit, feeling more relaxed than she had at any time since the calls had begun.

But, no sooner had she settled down in her chair, than the anonymous menace telephoned again.

"You shouldn't have gone to the police," he hissed, threateningly. "You're a naughty girl and naughty girls get punished."

Brenda knew that she had to keep him talking, so that the police would have enough time to trace the number that he was calling from.

"How do you know I've been to the police?" she asked. "Or are you just surmising?"

"I know everything about you," he continued. "You're also thinking of moving to Southport."

Brenda froze. She hadn't even told her daughters about her intention to move to Southport and wondered how on earth he could know so many details about her life.

"I don't know what you're talking about," she bluffed. "I wouldn't dream of leaving Liverpool."

"You're right! You won't be going anywhere!" he said, suddenly sounding even more aggressive and almost manic. "I'm going to pay you and your daughters a visit." At that point, the line went dead.

Thirty minutes later, two policemen called round to see Brenda.

"Did you manage to trace the number?" she asked eagerly. "Have you caught him?"

They followed her into the living room and suggested that she should sit down. They looked quite serious and were glancing nervously at each other, as though in search of moral support for the task which lay ahead.

"How long have you lived here, Mrs Gibson?" asked one of the policemen.

"Why?" she asked, curiously. "What's that got to do with the phone calls?"

"How long, Mrs Gibson?" he insisted.

"Eight years," she answered. "But why?"

The policeman who was speaking looked at his colleague with a somewhat puzzled expression on his face. The other policeman continued the explanation.

"We traced the number to this address!" he said, watching for Brenda's response. "It was traced to your own number!"

"What?" she retorted. "It's not possible. I've only got the one phone."

"We know," continued the policeman. "We checked our records and Alan McCarthy lived here fifteen years ago. He was cautioned several times by the police for making obscene phone calls to a middle-aged lady in Speke. In fact, he murdered her!"

"Oh! My God!" Brenda gasped. "And he's obviously out of prison now. I hope you're going to arrest him before he does any harm to me or my children."

The two policemen looked at each other, then turned towards her. There was a moment's silence before one of them spoke.

"That won't be possible," he said, solemnly. "You see, Mrs Gibson, Alan McCarthy is dead! He committed suicide shortly after he had killed the woman in Speke."

"I don't understand!" she stuttered. "But how …?"

"We don't understand it either, Mrs Gibson," interjected the policeman, who was now smiling. "But at least you can be sure of one thing, Alan McCarthy's not in any position to do you, or your family, any harm."

Brenda glanced at the policeman, still with a concerned look on her face.

"Are you absolutely sure about that? Because I'm not!"

The ghostly telephone calls continued right up until Brenda Gibson moved to another house. The people who bought the house from her also received the same ghostly calls for a period of about six months. Then, without any warning, they stopped completely. Maybe Alan McCarthy could not pay his telephone bill and had his phone cut off!

This sort of phenomenon is quite common and there are many recorded cases very similar to that of Brenda Gibson's.

The Dream

The phenomenon of precognition is the ability to dream of an event in the future, which then actually happens, and it is something that is experienced by more people today than we realise. Twenty years ago, in Russia, a study was made of the actual process of dreaming and a great deal of consideration was given to the various different types of dreams and their possible meanings. It was concluded that, whilst a lot of dreams appear to be quite vivid in the consciousness of the dreamer, only a minority of them actually possess any prophetic element. The majority of dreams, therefore, are quite often no more than the product of either over-indulgence, or an anxious mind. The studies revealed that, in nine out of ten cases of prophetic dreams, the dreams themselves contained impending dooms and disasters and only very rarely contained anything pleasant.

In the analysis of a dream, it is vitally important to consider the entire dream and not just individual details taken from it. The more lucid the dream, the more likely it is to possess some prophetic element, or association with the truth.

The following story is true and tells of a young mother's insecurities about her baby, which were so strong, that they produced strange happenings in a dream.

Carol Wilde and her husband, Don, had been trying for a baby for four years, without success. They had more or less resigned themselves to the fact that it was probably not going to happen and when Carol was told that she was pregnant, she just could not believe it and had to pinch herself just in case she was dreaming. She just couldn't wait to tell Don as soon as he came home from work and, to celebrate, they booked a table for two at the most expensive restaurant in town.

The date she had been given for the baby's arrival was 3 March but she had a strong feeling that it would come earlier. She did not know why exactly, but she just had a feeling that her baby would be in a great hurry to be born. When she was seven months into the pregnancy, she was sitting with her friend, Jean, talking about babies, when the doorbell rang.

Carol opened the door, expecting it to be Jean's little boy but, instead, she found a little old lady standing on the doorstep, clutching a basket.

"Buy a lucky charm, my dear?" asked the woman, whose kindly face was drawn and lined with age. Carol noticed that she was frail and poorly dressed and wondered why the lucky charms had not worked for her.

"Buy a lucky charm, my dear," the elderly woman said again, stepping closer to the door.

"I don't think so!" said Carol hesitantly, glancing at the cluster of golden coloured charms which the woman was holding out towards her. She was just about to close the door when, suddenly, she thought better of it.

"Just a minute," she said to the woman, leaving the door slightly ajar whilst she went inside to fetch her purse.

She reappeared to find the old woman waiting patiently on the step, obviously hoping for a sale.

"How much are they?"

"The animals are one pound fifty," she said quickly, "and the Lucky Imps are two pounds each."

Although Carol thought that the charms were quite expensive, she retrieved a five pound note from her purse and proffered it towards her.

"I'll take two Lucky Imps," she said, smiling, intending to give one to her friend.

The old woman's bony hands fumbled clumsily to remove two Lucky Imps from the bunch of charms tied together with a piece of string and handed them to Carol. As she took them from the old woman's hand, she noticed that she was staring intently at her.

"Your baby will be a little boy," she announced with a smile. "He will be extremely gifted and very dark, like his father."

She was wrong about the baby's gender, the scan had clearly shown that it was a girl, not that it really mattered to Carol. However, she did wonder how on earth the old woman knew that Don was dark. The old woman waited for a response from her and, when she did not say anything, she smiled.

"You've been told that the baby is a girl?"

Her statement surprised Carol even more and she now felt a little uneasy, in case the old woman was about to tell her something that she did not want to know.

"This baby will be marked with the cross of good fortune."

"What do you mean?" asked Carol anxiously. "Will he be alright?"

The old woman grinned reassuringly.

"He will be a healthy child. Be happy my dear."

As Carol had suspected, her baby did arrive early and was born on Wednesday 1 March 1995, at 7pm. To Carol and Don's great surprise it was a little boy and not a girl as predicted by the scan.

"The gender is sometimes very difficult to determine," said the midwife, "but the most important thing is that your baby's healthy."

The first thing Carol requested was for her son to be checked for any unusual birthmarks, as the old gypsy woman had prophesied.

"None at all," said the nurse. "Your baby has beautiful skin and really stunning dark hair."

Carol had always been sensitive and quite insecure. Up until the baby's arrival, her husband had been her whole world. Now, though, her new baby son was part of the scenario and Carol bonded with him almost immediately. She had never been so happy and was keen to take him home.

On her return home with her baby, Carol felt overwhelmed with emotion and kept recalling what the old gypsy woman had said to her.

"She was only trying to reward you for buying her charms," Don had said, in an effort to reassure his wife. "Anyway, everyone knows that gypsies have got the gift of the gab!"

Carol accepted his words and she snuggled down into her bed for the first time, with her baby in the cot beside her.

That night something woke her from her deep sleep. She caught sight of the old gypsy woman, accompanied by a young man, carrying her baby from the bedroom. She tried desperately to wake her husband, but he was sleeping too deeply. Carol followed the gypsies to the field where they were camping and watched in horror as they placed her baby in a crib covered with different coloured flowers. As she watched the gypsies from a safe distance, she witnessed some sort of ritual taking place. They appeared to be initiating her son in some sacred ceremony and she was overwhelmed with fear for his life.

She could hear her baby crying as the leader of the group took him from the crib and made some sort of a mark upon his body. Carol wanted desperately to cry out, but she knew full well that if she did, they might kill both her and her baby. She waited patiently for the chance to rescue her son and seized the opportunity when they left him unattended for a moment. She snatched him from the flower-strewn crib and sped away from the fire-lit encampment, up the grassy rise and into the street leading to her home. She attempted to flag down some passing cars, but they just sounded their horns for her to get out of the way. She could see the gypsies chasing angrily behind her and, with her baby son held close to her chest, she kept on running as fast as her legs would carry her.

She reached her door and fumbled clumsily with the handle, opening it just in time, as the gypsies passed through her garden gate and began making their way along the path. She closed the door quickly behind her and her baby began to cry … Carol opened her eyes to the sound of her baby crying in the cot next to her.

"A dream!" she sighed with relief, wiping beads of perspiration from her forehead with a tissue.

"What's that?" mumbled Don, sleepily. "Did you say something?"

"Go back to sleep," she smiled. "It's only the baby crying."

She lifted her son carefully from the cot and held him closely in her arms and realised that he needed changing. She took him into the spare room, so as not to awaken Don and laid him gently on his changing mat on top of the table by the window. As she undid his little top and began to remove it, she noticed something on his chest and bent down to take a closer look. She could not believe what she saw. On the left hand side of his chest there was a red cross in a half circle of green. Below the cross was written the word 'elegido', which is Spanish for 'chosen'. Carol rubbed the strange symbol gently with her fingertips and noted that it had been made with some sort of chalk and was easy to remove. She took a cloth and quickly wiped away all trace of it from her son's body.

She could not believe what had happened and did not know whether to feel proud or afraid. One thing that she was certain of, was that no one would ever believe her story, were she to tell it, not even her husband Don.

To Where the Narrow Road Forks

When John and Pat Rafferty first viewed the Victorian house in Ullet Road, they fell in love with it almost immediately. John's new job, with a firm in Edge Lane, had necessitated the move from Manchester to Liverpool. They were presently staying with Pat's parents in Childwall until they found somewhere permanent of their own. With two children already and now another one on the way, they needed a bigger house than the one they had sold in Manchester and they both agreed that 33 Ullet Road was perfect for their expanding family. It was 1950 and Liverpool had not yet recovered from the War. John had been promoted to a new position, which meant more money and far better prospects. Their baby was due in three months time, on 15 September, so it was extremely important that they found a house soon.

They had managed to save quite a bit of money over the years and they borrowed the rest from the bank. The only vice which John had, was an occasional flutter on the horses. He had always been quite lucky and had won over a thousand pounds just before they had moved from Manchester. They bought the house in Ullet Road and moved in within six weeks. Although the decor was not at all to their liking, the house itself was exactly what they had both wanted. The area was quite respectable and the large gardens back and front made it ideal for the children.

The whole family settled down very quickly in their new home and Pat gave birth to a little girl on 14 September, making the family complete.

When John came in from work one cold November night, he announced to Pat that he had to go to a farewell dinner for a work colleague, who was retiring at the end of the year.

"It's on the eighteenth of December," he told her. "It's being held at an hotel in Ormskirk and, unfortunately, it's for men only, so I'm afraid you can't come. I'm really not looking forward to it, but there's absolutely no way I can get out of it!"

The 18 December was a cold and frosty day with a threat of thick fog in the evening, according to the weather forecast. Although Ormskirk was not very far away, John was not looking forward to driving in such hazardous conditions, especially by himself. Although it was foggy by 4pm, it was not as bad as the weathermen had predicted and John had come home early from work so that he could take his time driving to Ormskirk. He was not really familiar with the route and so he wanted to leave in good time, just in case the weather got worse.

It took him over an hour to reach Ormskirk, by which time the fog was extremely thick and he could scarcely see the bonnet of the car, let alone the road in front of him. The headlights cast a feeble beam and only sufficed to reveal the thick, impenetrable grey fog all around him. He drove with his face as close to the windscreen as possible and he had reduced his speed to ten miles an hour. The concentration required made him feel hot and flustered and he undid his tie with a sigh of relief. He could never stand wearing anything tight around his neck. It was impossible to see any road signs or landmarks and he did not have a clue where he was, or even if he was actually still driving on the road at all. Pat's last words kept passing annoyingly through his mind, "only a fool would go out on a night like this", she had warned him and he had to admit that she was right. He was a fool and now he regretted not having made some excuse not to go. After all, he hardly knew Ted Jones and had only spoken to him on three occasions in all the time they had worked together.

Stopping his car at what he had estimated was the roadside, John got out to try and get his bearings and to see if there was anyone passing by who could tell him where exactly he was. Not surprisingly, there was absolutely no one around on such a night, but he had an idea that he was in the middle of the countryside. He thought he could hear cows some yards away and there was the familiar damp odour of farmland in winter, intermingled with the smell of the fog. By now, John had resigned himself to the obvious fact that he was not going to make it to the function and he just wanted to be back home with his wife and children, in front of the warm fire or, better still, tucked up in his bed. Instead, he was stuck in thick fog, in the middle of nowhere and had no clue about his exact position. He decided to drive a little further on and, if necessary, he would sleep in the car until the fog had lifted or even, perhaps, stay the night at a country inn, if he was fortunate enough to come across one.

He had driven for no more than five minutes, when he reached a spot where the fog appeared to be a little thinner. He could just about distinguish the narrow road he was driving along and noticed that he had reached a fork. Pausing for a moment, he decided almost immediately to take the right fork in the road and somehow had a strong feeling that he now knew exactly where he was going, as though he had been there before. The road passed through an extremely dark and ominous-feeling woodland and he was once again overwhelmed with the sensation of having been there before, even though he knew this was not the case.

Eventually he found himself parked at the gates of what looked like an old manor house and, as the gates had been left open, he decided to drive through them and along the winding driveway until the old house itself was reached. From the very moment that he had reached the fork in the road, he had been overwhelmed by feelings which he could only describe as déjà vu. Now the old manor house itself seemed uncannily familiar to him, even though he had never visited this part of the country before. As he climbed wearily from his car, he seemed to have a sense of 'knowing' exactly where he was. Even the five stone steps up to the ornately carved oak doors seemed so familiar and, for a moment, his thoughts drifted back to the days when the house was first built. He had always had an affinity with the historical period during which the house had been built and nurtured a strong desire to collect pieces of furniture from that time. Pat, however, had more modern tastes and despised anything that was older than she was, so he had never been able to indulge this passion.

John had intended to ask the people who lived in the house for some assistance, or perhaps they would allow him to stay there, at least until the fog had lifted sufficiently for him to resume his journey. As he ascended the stone steps, he could see that the old place was in darkness and was probably unlived in. He reached out for the heavy metal knocker and the door opened, with no more than a little shove. As he entered the hallway, he was immediately overwhelmed by the musty smells and cold damp atmosphere associated with empty houses and he quickly surmised that nobody had lived there for quite some time.

Before venturing further into the house, he called out to make quite certain that it was empty. His voice echoed through the darkness of the empty house and, although the old place was quite eerie, he did not feel uncomfortable or afraid in any way whatsoever.

He found an old oil lamp which still contained a small amount of oil and, after several attempts, he managed to light it. All the time he seemed to be guided by some deep-rooted instinct, as he systematically wended his way through the empty house from room to room. He seemed to be quite familiar with the architectural layout and was quite surprised to discover that he knew exactly where the kitchen was situated. He could not understand why the old house was so familiar to him, or why he was experiencing a strange feeling of excitement in the pit of his stomach. He was so preoccupied with his search, that he had quite forgotten the reason why he was there in the first place.

Unperturbed by his surroundings, he decided that he would find a comfortable chair in which to settle down for the night. Although the old manor had obviously been empty for some time, all the furniture was still in place, covered with white, protective dust sheets. John snuggled down on a large, plush settee and, in no time at all, had fallen fast asleep.

He woke up just before six o' clock the following morning and, although it was still fairly dark outside, he could see the moon shining through the window at the top of the stairs and therefore knew that the fog had cleared. His night spent in the unheated house had left him feeling stiff and chilled and he could not wait to get home. Pat would be worried sick and he would have to find a telephone box as soon as possible to let her know that he was alright.

The room was illuminated by the silvery light of the moon and he could now see the fireplace quite clearly. Its ornate surround was engraved with a family crest and the name, John Barrington Moore, was etched into its centre. John went cold as he read the name. It was so familiar and seemed to jog some ancient memory within him. His mind was flooded with images and thoughts of days gone by. He was sure that he had read somewhere that John Barrington Moore had been hanged for murder in the nineteenth century. He could not quite remember where exactly he had read it, but he definitely, somehow, recalled the name. This made him feel quite unsettled and he wanted to leave at once.

As soon as John was seated in his car and had started the engine, he could feel his heart pounding inside his chest. He turned the vehicle round in front of the house and accelerated quickly down the gravel driveway, glancing nervously in the mirror as he sped quickly through the gates, leaving the imposing old house behind him. The whole episode occupied his mind to such an extent on the way home, that he completely forgot to telephone Pat to let her know that he was safe and well.

John's stay in the old house had been the sole topic of conversation for over a week now and he knew that his wife did not believe one word of his story. And so, on a bright Sunday afternoon, two weeks after the New Year, he decided to take a drive with her and the children to find the old house. It was a beautiful clear day and, to John's great surprise, he was able to drive straight to it, without getting lost once.

He drove through the gates and along the winding driveway towards the front entrance, with a rush of excitement quickening his heart. He was looking forward to seeing the imposing edifice once again, this time in full daylight and he wanted to prove to Pat, once and for all, that he had been telling the truth. But he was in for a nasty shock. As the car emerged from the driveway and edged towards the front of the house, he could not believe what he was seeing. Before him was only the shell of a house, silhouetted against the clear blue sky; its fire charred walls now decaying beneath the winds of time.

"Some house!" scoffed Pat sarcastically. "And I suppose you're now going to tell me that this is not the place?"

John pulled the car to a halt and just sat in stunned silence, unable to respond to his wife's remark. Then somebody tapped on the side window and he turned his head to see an elderly man standing there smiling at him.

"Nice to see you again, Mr Barrington," the man grinned, with a sudden look of embarrassment as John turned to face him. " Oh! I do beg your pardon, Sir," he said. "I thought you were Mr Barrington Moore."

John felt an icy shiver pass right through him, as though someone had walked across his grave. He climbed out of the car, eager to speak to the man.

"I'm the gardener here, Sir," he said. "I've been looking after these gardens since I was a young man."

"The house ..." John stammered. "What's happened to the house?"

"Oh, the house was burnt down in the late nineteenth century," the old man answered.

John went even colder and could not believe the information he had just been given. He knew that he had stayed there on that foggy night and had looked around the old house and seen the fireplace with the inscription on its surround.

"That's not possible!" he replied, in a daze. "I came here ..."

He stopped suddenly to face the old house and the old man noticed the puzzled look on his face.

"John Barrington Moore murdered his uncle in a fit of rage," explained the old man. "He then set fire to the house. He was hanged six months later." The man paused for a moment, while John absorbed the information. But he had known that already. He had remembered it when he was looking at the fireplace. "You're the spitting image of the present Mr John Barrington Moore. The spitting image you are," the gardener went on.

John found the whole thing a little too bizarre to take in. He felt unable to tell Pat the whole incredible story, because he knew she would not believe a word of it.

"What was the name of the uncle who was murdered?" he asked.

"Charles Barrington Moore. He was quite wealthy and lived in this house which was owned by his nephew."

John was fascinated and wanted to find out all he could about the family.

"Why did he murder his uncle?"

"He threatened to cut his nephew out of his will," continued the old man. "John Barrington Moore was a gambling man and had lost all his money. He burnt the house down to cover his misdeeds."

The old gardener bade John farewell and made his way slowly back along the path towards the gardens at the rear of the house. John stood there for a moment, pensively watching the retreating figure. It was all coming back to him, image after powerful image, flooding his mind with memories that he was now somehow being forced to remember.

John had never believed in reincarnation, but this was all too much of a coincidence. He was being overwhelmed by strong emotions from the past and for the moment he felt as though he was living in two completely different ages.

"I am John Barrington Moore!" he muttered to himself. "I have returned ..."

His thoughts were sharply interrupted by Pat, who was calling him from the car.

"John, can we go now, the kids are starving and the baby's waking up!"

He climbed back into the car with a heavy sigh. He started the engine and turned in front of the house for the last time, before accelerating quickly down the long driveway and through gates, without glancing back once.

He was now certain that he was John Barrington Moore and that, for some reason, he had returned to the house which he had destroyed. John never returned to the house, for he had no desire to be hanged for the same crime twice!

The House that Sank

Many of the superstitions we hold today come from the legends and folklore handed down, through the generations, from bygone days. Most people have grown up with these traditions and perhaps received them as harsh warnings as a child. "Don't cut your nails on a Sunday, or the devil will take you!" my mother would always say. "Don't play cards on a Sunday, or you will play with the devil!" It is uncertain where exactly these superstitious sayings first originated, but they still carry a great deal of power even today.

Even though we may say it is all nonsense, the majority of people are still secretly afraid, or superstitious of certain things. Touching wood is one example, throwing salt over the shoulder is another. Most people avoid walking under a ladder and those who remember, will say, "white rabbit, white rabbit, white rabbit," when there is an 'r' in the month. But are we giving these superstitions more power over us, simply by continuing to practise them? Will the devil really come if we play cards on a Sunday? It is said that three men met their deaths when they ignored the warning of such a superstition.

There are, in fact, two recorded cases: one in Gronant, North Wales, and the other in Catherine Street, Liverpool, where flats have now been built to replace an old church.

In 1768, Jack Legg always looked forward to his friends calling in on him on a Friday night, to drink ale and play cards. They would stay in his cottage until the sun came up and all the ale had been drunk. Jack Legg's wife had left him because of his gambling and drunken ways and now, although he was in his mid-50s, he lived the life of a single man and was very rarely sober.

It was a Sunday night in the middle of February and there had been a snowstorm all over the Northwest. Jack Legg had backed up the fire with logs and stocked his larder with ale and eagerly awaited his friends, Tom Peet and Joe Mathews, who were due to arrive at around 9pm. As it was Jack Legg's birthday, they had decided to do some additional serious drinking on the Sunday as well as the customary Friday. Tom and Joe were both married with families and so they had had to come up with some good excuses, in order for them to be allowed out for a second night. Jack Legg was not a well-liked man and Tom and Joe were his only friends and had been since they were children together. Jack frequently became aggressive with drink and Tom and Joe knew exactly how to handle him.

"Bring plenty of money with you," Jack had warned. "I'm feeling lucky."

The three friends settled down to their bonus night of drinking, merriment and cards. It had been snowing all day long and the log fire roared up the chimney as Jack poured the ale and Joe dealt the cards. By the time that the clock on the mantelpiece struck midnight, the three of them were quite drunk. Tom had won most of the games and Jack was quite angry.

"You'll win it all back next time," slurred Joe. "It makes a change, Tom winning."

Jack was in the middle of pouring each man another pot of ale, when there was a knock on the door.

"Who the hell can that be at this time of night?" grunted Jack, staggering drunkenly to his feet.

"If it's my Beth," sniggered Tom, "tell her I'm not here."

They chuckled as Jack pulled back the door. On the step, shivering in the cold, was a young man wearing a black cape and a top hat. He was shivering and blue with cold and asked Jack if he could shelter for an hour from the snowstorm.

"Come in from the cold," said Jack, cordially, hoping to entice the young man into playing cards. "I hope you're a drinking man?"

The young man nodded and moved immediately towards the fire to warm his hands.

"What are you doing out on such a night?" asked Joe. "The devil himself wouldn't venture out on a night like this."

The young man smiled as he removed his cape and hung it carefully on the back of the door.

"I've been to meet my friend," he said, "but he wasn't there."

"No wonder!" interjected Tom. "The weather's awful and it's bound to get worse. You've come to the right place, anyway lad. We've got plenty of ale and money to lose."

Jack gestured for the young man to pull up his chair closer to the table.

"I hope you've got plenty of money with you?"

The young man nodded and retrieved a leather pouch from the pocket of his waistcoat which was bulging with coins. He ostentatiously pulled the pouch open and emptied a pile of gold coins onto the table. Jack and his friends looked at each other in disbelief.

"I hope you can play cards?" Jack continued. "But we only play for small stakes."

"Yes I can," he said, resting his elbows on the table. "I enjoy a good game of cards, particularly when there's money involved."

Jack poured him a pot of ale.

"I hope you're not a professional gambler," he joked, "we're just simple folk who enjoy the social activity of a game or two of cards."

He looked sideways at his friends and winked slyly.

Jack invited the young man to deal the first hand and the three men watched intently as he dealt the cards clumsily onto the table like an amateur. But he immediately went on to anger Jack by winning the first two games.

"Beginner's luck!" he snarled, trying his best to intimidate the young man. "You'll not win any more."

The stranger was not at all worried, nor would he allow himself to be intimidated in any way, which infuriated Jack even more. In fact, the young stranger kept on winning, until Jack's money had gone.

"I'll give you my IOU," said Jack scribbling on a scrap piece of linen. "Here!"

"You have no money," said the stranger. "What good is your IOU?"

At that, Jack slammed his fist onto the table.

"You've taken all my money!" he mumbled incoherently. "You've got to give me a chance to win some of it back."

The young man sat back on his chair and stared seriously at Jack across the table.

"I repeat what I've just said, you have no money."

Jack was furious but was restrained by Joe's hand.

"I'll win your money back for you, Jack," he said reassuringly. "Just leave it to your friends."

Tom shuffled the cards and dealt the next game, accidentally dropping a card onto the floor. He stooped to retrieve it from beneath the table and was horrified to discover that the young man had cloven hooves instead of feet. He leapt up, banging his head on the table as he did so and made a dash for the door, leaving Jack and Joe sitting there completely bewildered.

"It's the devil," Tom shrieked, as he tried desperately to pull the door open but, for some reason, it would not budge.

The young man grinned sardonically, the grin slowly turning into evil laughter. Tom's two friends helped him to open the door and, with a great deal of effort, it swung wide open. But the cottage had somehow sunk into the ground and the doorway was blocked with earth, preventing their escape. They turned to look at the young man and he had metamorphosed into the demonic form that he really was. His insane laughter echoed around the walls of the small cottage and he screamed out the most horrible, blood-curdling cries they had ever heard.

"You are mine!" he cackled. "I have won your souls."

Joe Mathews is believed to have somehow escaped to tell the horrible tale, but died four weeks later from some unknown malady. The roof of the house was discovered the following day and, when it was excavated, Jack Legg and Tom Peet were found sitting rigidly upright on their chairs at the table, both stone dead, with a look of frozen horror on their faces. No trace of anyone else was found in the cottage.

A church was later constructed on the site of the submerged cottage but was then demolished some years later and, in its place, some flats were built. Several people walking home in the early hours of the morning have claimed to have heard the sound of insane laughter echoing down Catharine Street …

The Séance

Long gone are the days when the highlight of the week was the parlour séance and the family would gather around a table holding hands and asking, "is there anybody there?" Today, the phenomenon of the spiritualist séance has been completely transformed and brought right up to date. There is no longer any great need to sit in the dark, holding hands, as the more modern approach to spirit communication is now without any great mystery or secrecy and is very often produced with great ease.

It was not difficult for the charlatan medium to exploit those who attended the Victorian séance and to use trickery to produce the various phenomena such as the 'flying trumpet', or the levitating table. This story, however, is about a well-respected medium who lost his gift and had to resort to deceit to maintain his status as the leader of the séance. The story actually took place around the early 1950s, in a house in Dovecot. The medium in question had reached his mature years and was regarded as one of the veteran mediums of the day. When he began to lose his psychic abilities, he felt compelled to fabricate them in order to maintain his popularity. I have obviously changed the name of the medium in question, so as to avoid any embarrassment to his family.

George Bowler devoted his whole life to spiritualism and had run the 'home' circle, as it was called, for the previous 25 years. Although there had been one or two additions to the circle members, the majority of them were the same and these were all equally dedicated to the circle's activities and attended religiously every Friday night at 8pm prompt.

There were ten members of the circle, including George, and each one of them was quite content to simply give energy to him, without any thoughts of developing paranormal abilities for themselves. They usually hoped to witness the séance trumpet, sounding with its disembodied voice and flying quickly around the circle but, as yet, this phenomenon had not occurred. There had been the odd knock on the table, but no one was really certain whether or not that was a paranormal event, or simply somebody accidentally knocking the table with a foot. Nobody in the circle would admit to it, so the phenomenon was always attributed to the guide of the circle, just letting everybody know that he was there.

However, the highlight of the week was the production of apports (objects brought on the scene at a spiritualistic séance by no visible agency) from George's mouth. This phenomenon involved small items of cheap jewellery, or lucky charms being produced, almost by magic, for selected members of the circle. This was done primarily as a show of appreciation from the spirit world and the person who was fortunate enough to receive one, believed that the small item just appeared from nowhere via George's mouth. As the room was in total darkness, no one ever really knew what was going on and it was just accepted, by most of those present, that

George Bowler was genuine and really did produce these items from his mouth. However, one of the sitters became increasingly suspicious as to the medium's honesty and decided to put the whole process to the test. Eddy Maddox knew that the séance room was always kept locked and was only unlocked 20 minutes before the proceedings actually started. On this occasion he purposely arrived early at George Bowler's house and sat talking to him over a cup of tea. Waiting for the appropriate moment, he asked if it was alright to use his bathroom.

"Help yourself," he replied. "You don't have to ask."

Eddy went directly to the séance room at the back of the house. The door was open as he had expected and so, checking that there was not anybody in there, he crept inside as quietly as he could. Eddy knew that if George Bowler was using trickery, there had to be a secret place in which he kept the apports. He had to act quickly, in case anyone heard him moving about in the room. He lowered himself to his hands and knees and felt around under the medium's chair. Just as he had expected, there was a small box stashed underneath the seat of the ornately carved chair in which he found several small items, a couple of rings, brooches and some tiny charms. George Bowler was faking it alright, just as he had suspected and now he knew that he must expose him as a charlatan to all the other members of the group.

Eddy frantically searched his pockets for something with which to replace the pieces of jewellery and all that he could find was a packet of jelly babies. Smiling mischievously, he removed the apports and emptied the jelly babies into the box, before firmly securing it beneath the seat of the chair. He carefully placed the chair back into position then tiptoed from the room, filled with a feeling of satisfaction.

The séance began, as usual, with a prayer, then they sat through the usual philosophical debate conducted by George Bowler, followed by a period of hushed silence. Although the séance was conducted in complete darkness, Eddy's eyes had gradually become accustomed to the absence of light and could just about distinguish George's movements. He could see that he was ready to produce the apports and he waited patiently for it to happen. He knew George had to put them into his mouth first of all and wondered exactly what he would do when he tasted the jelly babies. However, to Eddy's delight, on this occasion George had made some changes to the whole procedure. Instead of putting them into his mouth, he could see him throwing the apports onto the table, hoping that everybody believed that they had been materialised by the spirit world. The séance was concluded with a prayer and everyone, except Eddy, that is, eagerly reached across the table to retrieve their apport. "Jelly babies!" they all cried simultaneously and Eddy sniggered with mischievous delight at the horrified expression on George's face.

"What do you think, George?" he asked, sarcastically. "Do they think you've got a sweet tooth then?"

The poor man's face was purple with embarrassment and, for one brief moment, his eyes suddenly locked on to Eddy and his lips tightened and quivered with a mixture of anger and shame. He would obviously incriminate himself if he spoke out against him and he was left anxiously wondering whether Eddy would tell the others, or just keep it to himself. Although he had initially intended to expose the medium as a charlatan, he now felt quite sorry for him and realised his dilemma, now that he had lost his gift completely.

But, for him, the Friday night séance had nothing more to offer and this would definitely be the last time that he would be having anything to do with George Bowler. He rose to his feet and made his excuses to leave.

"Have a jelly baby, George," he said with a smile, dropping one onto George's lap. "I've always been a little bit wary of taking sweets from strangers. After all, you never know where they've been, do you?"

The Stranger

There is an old saying that everybody has a twin somewhere in the world, but we never think for one moment that perhaps that twin could possibly be a ghost! Some stories are more difficult to believe than others and yet, occasionally, the most ridiculous tale turns out to be true. Through my work I have encountered many different experiences, but none so strange and unusual as the true story I am about to relate.

Bill Young had been divorced and now lived alone with his cat, Jake, in a terraced house in Wellington Avenue, Wavertree. He had retired from his work on the docks two years ago in 1970 and, although he had lots of friends, he really did enjoy his own company and spent quite a lot of time by himself. He occupied most of his spare time reading historical novels and he often felt an affinity with the Victorian period of history, secretly believing that he had somehow lived in that time. Bill was not in any way a dreamer, he was quite practical and down to earth. However, he did believe in the concept of reincarnation and always felt that Jake was the reincarnation of a cat he had once had as a child.

On Thursday nights Bill would meet his friend, Tommy Whitehead, at the Waldeck pub on Lawrence Road. Tommy was interested in the same things as Bill and so he really looked forward to these nights. Bill was walking home from the pub around 11 o'clock one October night, when he noticed that there was a very distinctive crescent moon in the sky and stood for a moment by the entry, just past the off licence, gazing at the eerie looking clouds passing in front of it. He had eventually begun walking down Wellington Avenue, when he thought he heard someone calling his name in a low voice. It was so faint that he could not be certain that he had not imagined it. But it came again, a little louder this time, causing him to walk back to the entry to try and discover who it was. It was quite dark and there was no way that he was going to be enticed into the entry.

"Who is it?" he called, screwing his eyes up to see through the darkness. "Who's there?"

He could just about distinguish a shadowy figure moving in the entry towards him and he waited for whoever it was to come into the light. But the figure remained firmly in the shadows and beckoned for him to walk into the entry to meet him. Bill just shrugged and walked off down the street towards his front door. He felt a little uneasy and turned to see if he was being followed. The street was deserted but he could see that the figure had emerged from the entry and now had his eyes on him as he approached his house. Bill stood for a moment watching the figure standing by the entry. He thought it was quite strange that whoever it was did not wave or call out to him.

"Who the hell is that?" he muttered to himself.

The figure appeared to be attired in a long, cloak-like garment and had straggly, shoulder length hair. Bill decided that it must be his neighbour's son playing a joke on him.

"Bloody nutcase!" he cursed dismissively, as he walked through the gate and up the path to his front door.

The next day the incident was still on his mind and he told one of his neighbours about it. She seemed quite surprised that Bill had not heard such stories before.

"It's the ghost of a man," she said seriously. "He's been seen many times. He always calls you by name. It's quite spooky really, he seems to know everyone's name in the neighbourhood. Mrs Jones never walks past that entry at night."

He had looked so real to Bill and he wondered if the woman was just exaggerating a little, or pulling his leg. He did not really believe in ghosts and had politely listened to his neighbour, so as not to appear too rude.

Over the following few days, he mentioned the figure to a few people in the street and was amazed to find that they all confirmed the same story.

"He always calls you by name," they said.

By the time the next Thursday came round, Bill invited his friend back to his house after closing time and had completely forgotten about the figure in the entry. Lost in conversation, the two men passed the entry and it was not until they had reached Bill's house that he suddenly remembered about the ghostly figure. Tommy had already gone through the gate and Bill paused for a moment to glance back to check if the figure was there and, sure enough, he could clearly see the silhouette of the slender man, with his long cape and scraggy hair blowing in the wind. He felt more than a little spooked now that he had been told it was a ghost. He had mentioned it to Tommy over a pint in the Waldeck but he had just laughed and disregarded the story completely. Bill decided that he could now see the figure for himself.

"Tommy, lad," he called to his friend. "Come and take a look at this."

Tommy shuffled his way tiredly back to the gate and glanced in the direction that Bill was indicating but the figure of the man had disappeared completely.

"What are you pointing at?" he asked Bill. "I can't see anything."

"It was the odd-looking ghost I was telling you about," said Bill, somewhat puzzled by the man's disappearance. "He was there a minute ago, I saw him standing by the entry."

"Come on, Bill lad, I'm dying to use your toilet," said Tommy impatiently, disregarding Bill's concerned tones and retreading his steps towards the front door. Tommy had drunk too much whiskey, so Billy insisted that he stay the night.

Bill saw the unusual figure again several times after that night and, on each occasion, the mysterious man had called his name. He was becoming extremely disturbed about the whole thing and was even considering moving house.

It was Saturday night and Bill had been invited to a wedding anniversary party at the Labour Club on Picton Road. He had had quite a lot to drink and was in an extremely argumentative mood. After a disagreement with a woman over spilling her drink, he left the party around midnight and made his way home down Bishopgate

Street. The chip shop on Grosvenor Road was still open, so he stopped to get some fish and chips for his supper. He noticed two young lads watching him with some interest from the shop doorway opposite the chip shop but, at the time, thought nothing more about it. When he left the shop, holding his supper securely in his hands, he was aware that they began to follow him. Every time that he quickened his pace, he noticed that they, too, seemed to hurry to keep up with him. He eventually reached Lawrence Road by St Bridget's Church and was relieved to see quite a few other people making their way home. He glanced back to check if he was still being trailed, but was relieved to find that the two lads had gone. He relaxed a little and began to walk at a slower pace but still kept looking all around him to make sure he was safe.

Sure enough, as he turned the corner to walk into Wellington Avenue, the two lads were standing by the entry, obviously lying in wait for him. He knew he could not turn back now and had to keep on walking down his road. When he reached the entry and tried to pass them by, one of them stood directly in front of him, blocking his way.

"What the hell are you playing at?" Bill demanded, trying his best not to show them that he was afraid.

He had just pushed the young lad out of the way, when the second one punched him to the ground. They were both about to set on him, when the by now familiar voice called out from the entry.

"Bill!"

The voice seemed to echo around the three of them and caused his attackers to stop in their tracks and look in the direction of the entry. As they stared into the darkness, a shadowy figure appeared and the two lads took in the long cape and shoulder length hair and for a moment did not move. The ghostly form raised its arms and shouted out their names, slowly and deliberately.

"Keith Shaw and Kevin Long," it boomed.

The two lads looked wide-eyed at each other, then fled at top speed down Wellington Avenue in the direction of Smithdown Road. Bill pulled himself to his feet, dusted himself down and then retrieved his supper, still neatly wrapped, from the pavement. He was still quite drunk and very shaken by his ordeal, but he now felt quite brave and wanted to take a closer look at the ghostly figure who had come to his rescue, just in time.

He staggered into the entry towards the wall where the strange figure was standing and was suddenly overwhelmed with fear. He turned to move away, but it was too late, a ghostly hand was upon him almost immediately. It was icy cold and Bill could feel his whole body trembling with fear as the hand pulled him closer. The man stepped forward and the moon shone a beam of light directly onto his face. Bill looked into his eyes as the hand loosened its grip. He could not believe what he saw. As he looked at the ghostly face he was looking at himself, as if in a mirror. He screamed out, "No! No!" and ran from the entry as fast as he could, not stopping until he had opened his front door and was safely inside.

The ghostly figure was never seen again and it was said that whoever touched upon him that dark night would have come face to face with themselves.

Before that night, Bill Young had been proud of the fact that there was very little grey in his hair. The next day, however, his thick mane had turned completely white.

Although the ghostly figure has never been seen again since that night, there are those who are quite sure that he is still there in the entry, lurking somewhere in the dark shadows ...

The Grim Reaper of Hayfield Street

Frank Lindon had always been close to his mother, Margaret, and was devastated when he learned that she was suffering from lung cancer and the prognosis was not good. She was a widow and lived with her sister Edie, in Wavertree and Frank lived in Hayfield Street, Anfield, a few miles away. Margaret had grown up in Anfield and she had often told her son stories of the days when she was a child playing in the streets where he now lived with his wife, Jean, and two daughters, Barbara and Jenny.

Frank and his family had only been living in the corner house in Hayfield Street for six months and had quickly settled into the friendly community. The neighbours had been very helpful when they moved in and even offered to help carry furniture up the narrow staircase to the bedrooms. It was so friendly that Frank and Jean felt as though they had always lived there and the girls even looked forward to going to school for the first time.

Frank's mother appeared to respond to her treatment and it looked as though she was going into remission. He knew he could not have his mother forever, but he just prayed that she would survive for a few more years, if only to see her granddaughters grow up.

It was a warm Saturday evening in July 1986 and Frank and Jean had taken the children to spend the evening with their grandmother in Wavertree. She appeared to be in good spirits and was talking about the future with a positive attitude. Frank could see that there had been some improvement, if only in her psychological state and he began to feel cautiously optimistic. He worked at Fords and was on the early shift that Sunday, so they left his mother's at about nine o'clock so that he could have a shower and an early night. At about three o'clock the next morning, something woke him from his intense sleep. Jean also was quite restless and eventually opened her eyes.

"What's the matter, love?" she asked, putting a comforting hand on his back.

"Something woke me up," he said, rubbing his eyes "I know it's ridiculous but it sounded like horses' hooves on the cobbles outside."

"What cobbles?" laughed Jean. "There aren't any cobbles on the street. You must have been dreaming. There aren't any horses around here either for that matter."

As he slowly came to his senses, he suddenly realised what he had been saying.

"You're right, love," he whispered, swinging his legs to the floor from beneath the bed covers. "I must've been dreaming. But I'll just take a look anyway."

He crossed over towards the window and peeped through the curtains, but the street was deserted, just as he had suspected.

"Come back to bed, love," said Jean in a reassuring voice. "You're probably worried about your mum."

"I suppose so!" he yawned and climbed back into bed and pulled the covers over himself again. "You go back to sleep," he said to Jean. "I'll just lie here for a while."

The night passed very slowly and Frank had not slept at all by the time the alarm clock went off at five o'clock and he climbed wearily out of bed.

"I'll get up when you've had your shower," Jean said, still half asleep. "I'll make you some breakfast."

"No," said Frank, "you stay in bed, I'm not going into work today. I've decided to take a few weeks off. The doctor will give me a note I'm sure."

This was not like her husband and Jean was immediately concerned about him and knew that he was more worried about his mother than he was prepared to admit.

The following night Frank and Jean stayed up until the early hours talking. The girls were fast asleep and the streets outside were quiet. Eventually, Jean yawned and stretched her arms above her head.

"I'm tired now, love, I think I'll go up."

Frank agreed that it was late and decided to join her. But again, at around three o'clock, he was woken up by the sound of horses' hooves on a cobbled street. He nudged Jean to listen and they both lay there in the darkness. It was silent for a few moments and then they both distinctly heard the sound of a horse, trotting across a cobbled surface. They sprang out of bed simultaneously and looked through the window into the dimly-lit street, not in any way prepared for the sight which greeted their eyes. In the street below was a black, plumed horse pulling an ornate Victorian funeral carriage and a man, dressed smartly in black with a top hat, leading the horse by its reins. They both shivered as the whole image faded into nothingness when the carriage reached the corner of the street by their house. Frank immediately switched on the light and sat on the bed in stunned silence.

"So, I wasn't dreaming after all!" he said, after a while. "What do you suppose it was?"

"I don't know," answered Jean, equally bewildered. "There must have been an undertaker's close by."

They both replayed the whole ghostly scene over and over in their minds. Frank was the first to speak.

"Let's get back into bed," he said, trying to dismiss the whole experience from his mind. "Don't know about you, but I'm absolutely shattered."

"Yeah, me too," responded Jean. "We'll talk about it in the morning. Maybe one of the neighbours can throw some light on it."

The first neighbour whom Jean asked about the incident was Kate Mellor who lived next door. She had lived there for 30 years and had to admit that she had neither seen, nor heard, anything remotely ghostly in all that time.

"Although they do say there's a ghost in number twenty-six," she told Jean. "But I don't know really."

The following night, Frank and Jean were half expecting the ghostly visitation again. They sat up in bed talking until well after midnight but, at that point, they were both so tired that they fell asleep and did not wake up again until the following morning at eight o'clock.

A few days passed by and then Frank's mother had been taken into hospital for more tests. That night the two of them were woken at about three o'clock by the same sound of a horse trotting across a cobbled surface. They both peered nervously at the now familiar scene through the curtains and, because the moonlight shone quite brightly, they could see the figure of the man leading the horse quiet clearly. This time, the horse and funeral carriage stopped almost outside their house. Kate Mellor had told Jean to ring her the next time they saw the ghostly apparition, but they were both so mesmerised by the scene outside their window, that they could not bring themselves to move from their position. The ghostly appearance remained a little longer on this occasion, before eventually evaporating, just as before, into nothingness.

Frank and Jean were completely unsettled until daylight shone through their bedroom curtains once again. Jean could not help thinking that the apparition was in some way connected with Frank's mother and he could not get the mental image out of his mind and it left him with a morbid, oppressive feeling, which stayed with him all day.

Two weeks passed by, during which time they had seen the phantom horse and carriage several times and, on each occasion, it had remained a little longer than the time before. By now, both Frank and Jean were totally exhausted and fell fast asleep each night as soon as they had climbed into bed. At three o'clock one morning they were both woken up with a start by three heavy knocks on their bedroom door. Thinking that it was one of the girls, Frank sprang quickly out of bed but there was no one there. He crept into his daughters' room and found that they were fast asleep. By the time that he arrived back in the bedroom, Jean was sitting bolt upright in bed, looking startled.

"Shush!" she murmured, staring straight ahead, with her finger pressed to her lips. "Listen!"

They could hear the horse trotting across the cobbles and they both crossed over to the window and looked through the curtains. The carriage had stopped outside their front door and they could now see a coffin on it for the first time, covered in flowers. Seconds later, the phantom funeral carriage had disappeared completely, leaving Frank and Jean feeling shaken and wondering if it was some sort of omen.

From experience they knew that sleep was impossible, so they were just on their way downstairs to make a cup of tea when the telephone rang. They looked at each other, expecting the worst. Frank's brother, Roger, was on the other end of the line.

"Mum's dead!" he said solemnly. "She died at three o'clock."

But Frank and Jean already knew …

Welcome Home, Walter Crone

Many soldiers returned from overseas after the Second World War with far more than physical wounds. Quite a lot of those who had been prisoners of war were left with broken spirits and mental scars which made it difficult for them to integrate into society on their return. The psychological damage which they had suffered was often irreparable and very often destroyed the whole fabric of their lives. Many turned to drink and the majority encountered difficulties in their relationships.

This story is about one man's return from the Japanese war camps and how he coped when he discovered that the torture to which he was subjected in Camp 11, had caused him to have paranormal abilities. It is a true story and the man in question died in 1998. Because many of his family are still alive, his name has been changed.

Walter Crone had spent three years in a Japanese prisoner of war camp and was now on his way home to Wavertree. Although he still bore the obvious physical wounds sustained through the systematic torture inflicted upon him by his Japanese captors in Camp 11, there were also the invisible wounds that no one else could see and only he could feel; the emotional pain and damage that was deeply embedded in his brain and which was with him every moment of every day, as a constant reminder of his ordeal. This emotional torment just would not go away. Even in sleep, there was no escape, no peace whatsoever.

He sat in the back of the limousine that had picked him up at Lime Street Station, unaware of the route upon which he was travelling and completely oblivious to the destruction which Liverpool had sustained during the air raids whilst he had been away. His eyes were focused on no particular point and, although he was apparently looking, he most certainly did not see anything at all. The driver was talking to him, but his words amounted to nothing more than a cacophony of mumbled sounds in Walter Crone's ears. He just wanted to be silent and left alone.

"I suppose you'll be glad to get home to your family?" said the driver, trying to be pleasant. "Have you got any children?"

It soon became blindingly obvious that his passenger did not want to speak and so he left him alone with his thoughts.

It had been a long time since Walter had actually spoken his own name. He had grown quite used to introducing himself as Private Crone 5933684 and now he must discipline himself to get out of that habit.

As the limousine turned the corner into Callow Road, the driver could immediately see the reception awaiting Walter. The sign across the street read, 'WELCOME HOME WALTER CRONE' and the crowds had turned out to endorse the message. Halfway down the road, tables had been laid out with drink and food and when the crowd spied the car approaching, they began to cheer and shout out, "Here he is!" Walter's wife and two teenage sons waited excitedly at the roadside to greet him as the limousine pulled to halt at the kerb. A man pulled the door open to welcome Walter but he just sat in the back of the limousine, staring vacantly at the faces waiting to greet him, with a look of sadness and confusion in his eyes, but with no recognition.

"Welcome home, Walter lad," grinned the man, thrusting his hand into the car for Walter to shake. "It's me, Vinny Hague. You remember me, don't you?"

Walter climbed nervously from the back of the limousine, as if in a daze, and Betty, his wife, immediately threw her arms around him and cried with joy. But Walter Crone felt empty inside and showed no feeling, but then he came to his senses a little and managed to mumble his first, almost incoherent words.

"Er, hello, love. It's good to be home."

They embraced each other and Walter felt the tears suddenly streaming into his eyes.

"It's so good to be home," he said again. "It's so good to be home."

His mother and brother John were there also and the whole reunion was charged with emotion.

Although he was definitely glad to be home and free of the horrors of Camp 11, Walter did not feel like celebrating. A lot of his friends had died out there and now he just wanted to forget but he already knew that was impossible. Betty instantly saw that he was extremely unsettled by all the fuss and so she took him into the house where it was quiet. At first the house felt a little strange to Walter, he had been so used to his hut in Camp 11. But as his eyes wandered round the cosy domestic scene, he was reassured that nothing had changed and everything was just as he had remembered it.

The weeks passed by and Walter slowly began to settle down once again to family life. The children were only young when he went to fight in Burma and so it took some time for them to come to terms with the fact that their father had come home at last. Very soon, Walter Crone, the hero, became simply Walter Crone from Callow Road. It was not that people had forgotten what he had been through, it was more that everyone wanted to get on with their lives now and forget all the atrocities which had happened in the War. His readjustment to everyday life was made harder by the difficulties he encountered in finding a job. All his efforts met with the same response: "Really appreciate what you lads went through, but business is quite poor at the moment. Try again in twelve months time", or words to that effect.

Walter could feel himself slipping further and further into depression. He had already lost most of his confidence and was now finding it very difficult to cope. He had always been physically strong and mentally quite disciplined. Whilst a prisoner of war he had deliberately worked on his mind, to prevent it from becoming sluggish and weak. In the process, he had achieved far greater things and he had even discovered that he possessed telepathic powers and could actually read people's minds. The trauma of being a prisoner in Camp 11 in some way aided the development of these powers and Walter had noticed that since he had returned home, his telepathic abilities appeared to be much stronger and far more efficient. But it bothered him that he could actually 'see' what people were thinking about and sometimes he wished it would all go away.

One day, Walter's wife had gone shopping on nearby Lawrence Road and he was sitting quietly in the living room thinking about the events of the past few years, when he heard a woman calling his name. He thought he must have left the front door open, so he went into the hallway to check. Although it was closed, a few moments later the voice came again. He put his hands to his ears to block out the sound but he could still hear the voice, whispering inside his head.

"Walter," said the voice softly. "It's your grandmother, May."

He was worried that he was going mad and dropped down on the chair by the fire with his heart racing, feeling decidedly shaky.

"Don't be frightened, dear," the voice said, reassuringly. "I want to help you."

Walter had never known his grandmother, she had died just before he was born, 42 years ago. But he was still not too sure and decided to question the voice in an attempt to prove, or disprove, its claim. He had to ask a question to which he himself did not know the answer. This was the only way he could be certain that the voice was not originating in his own mind. He knew very little about Grandma May, his mother's mother and so he decided to ask a question to which only his mother would know the answer.

"What road did you live in when my mother was born?" he asked.

At first there was only silence and Walter began to think it was all in his imagination after all. But then the voice came again.

"Bective Street, off Earl Road," she answered.

"What was the name of your husband and what name did everyone know him by?"

Walter knew quite well that he was named after his grandfather, but his grandfather also had a nickname that Walter never knew.

"Which one?" the voice laughed. "I was married twice. A tram killed my first husband, just after the First World War. His name was Tom. I was only married to him for twelve months. My second husband was Walter, your grandfather. Everyone called him Shimmy and, funnily enough, I never knew why."

Walter took the opportunity to ask numerous questions and just hoped that nobody could hear him. He could not wait to check answers with his mother and, to his surprise, she confirmed that all the details were correct.

"Why do you suddenly want to know all these things?" she had asked.

Walter had told her he was interested in the family tree and this answer seemed to satisfy her.

The voice of his grandmother returned almost every day and her communications seemed to motivate Walter in some way and give him hope for the future, but he decided not to tell anybody about her voice, just in case they thought he was going mad.

A few weeks had gone by and Walter was sitting in the front parlour, writing a letter to a soldier friend, when he noticed some funeral cars pulling into the road and stopping a few doors away. He had heard that old Mr Beckson had recently died but had not realised that his funeral was due to take place that day. He sat quietly for a few moments, watching the proceedings through the window. He used to like Charlie Beckson and his wife Molly and, as they had always been inseparable, he wondered how she would cope now that her husband had gone.

His thoughts were drifting along in this vein, when he heard another voice inside his head. This time it was a man speaking to him and Walter immediately recognised the voice as that of Charlie Beckson.

"It's me Walter, Charlie."

Walter sat bolt upright amazed by the whole phenomenon.

"I don't believe this!" he retorted. "I'm sitting here watching …"

"You're watching my funeral," interrupted the voice. "I know, I can see you."

Walter turned his head nervously to glance behind him, but there was nobody there.

"I know it sounds stupid," continued Walter, "but how are you, Charlie?"

He could hear Charlie chuckling to himself.

"I'm fine, Walter lad. A lot better than I was. Tell Molly I'm OK. Tell her how I came to visit you. She'll believe you. Tell her I'm with David, our son, and together we'll look after her."

Walter went quiet as he saw the funeral cars slowly pulling away from the door one by one.

"I've got to go now, Walter," said the voice. "Please do that for me, she needs some encouragement right now."

After worrying about it for some time, Walter decided that he had to deal with the task in hand and the very next day he called on Molly, who now lived alone. He told her the whole story from beginning to end, firstly about his grandmother and then about her husband, Charlie. He told his story so convincingly that she believed him without question and she wept with a mixture of sadness and joy. At least now she knew her husband Charlie still existed somewhere and that he was watching over her.

Charlie came to Walter frequently to speak about his wife Molly and to send messages to her and he got quite accustomed to the sound of Charlie's voice. Then there were communications from other so-called 'dead' people, who seemed to delight in the fact that they could talk to Walter.

Just before Christmas, Charlie came to Walter sounding very excited. Walter, however, was not prepared for what Charlie had to say this time.

"I just thought you'd like to know," he said, "Molly will be joining me tomorrow night."

Walter could not believe what he was hearing.

"What?" he gulped, taking in the enormity of what he had just heard. "What on earth do you mean?"

"Molly's coming home!" Here Charlie paused for a moment. "She's not been too well for a long time. It's her heart."

"But why are you so pleased?" asked Walter, concerned. "Your wife is going to die!"

"She's coming home to me," he answered, knowing it was difficult for Walter to understand. "She's very lonely and she misses me. We'll be together again."

Charlie then said goodbye to him and thanked him for all his kindness.

At nine o'clock the following evening, Walter's wife broke the news to him about Molly.

"They found Molly Beckson lying in the hallway dead!" she announced, expecting some reaction from him but Walter was not surprised and just nodded.

"She's better off," he mumbled quietly, sounding unconcerned. "At least she's with Charlie now."

The news somehow got out that Walter Crone had psychic abilities and people began calling on him for help. He even used his abilities to locate a young girl who had gone missing. He told the police to look for her in Garmoyle Road, where they would find her, safe and well, with a friend. He was even able to give the police the exact number on the door. Unfortunately, Walter Crone was also able to foresee such distressing events as the sudden death of his own wife, Betty, two months before it actually happened in 1985.

In January 1998, Walter confided in his closest friend that he had recently had a premonition about his own death.

"I am going to die on my own birthday this year," he announced, in a matter-of-fact tone of voice.

He made quite certain that all his affairs were in order and then, as he had predicted, on 11 November of that year, he passed away suddenly in his sleep.

Walter Crone was undoubtedly one of the finest mediums in the world. Although his psychic abilities had seemingly developed as a result of all the trauma in Camp 11, he himself eventually had to admit that his paranormal abilities had probably always been there from birth, at least potentially.

The number eleven had always figured prominently in Walter's life. He was born and died on the eleventh day of the eleventh month, he was incarcerated in Camp 11 during the War, he lived at number 11 and all the digits in his army number added up to the number eleven, numerologically.

The Poltergeist

In 1986 I was asked by another medium to accompany her to a house in Hartington Road, Toxteth, where a poltergeist was causing havoc to the family that lived there. Although I had encountered many poltergeists during my work as an investigative medium, I had never experienced anything like the phenomena I was to encounter at the old house in Hartington Road.

Upon our arrival at the Pritchard's home, we were greeted by Jim, a slightly built, frail man, who stood no higher than five feet, two inches tall. My immediate impression was that he looked quite tired and sickly and appeared to be of a nervous disposition.

As we entered the premises and followed the man down the hallway, I noticed that a strange odour permeated our route into the back living room, where his wife was lying, sprawled out on the settee. The unusual odour was more prevalent in the room where she was lying and it was a smell which strongly reminded me of another poltergeist location which I had come across some years before.

After he had introduced me to his wife, Jim quickly and unobtrusively left the room. The woman was extremely obese and was obviously incapable of moving from her prone position on the settee. Apparently she was disabled and suffered from a variety of ailments, all of which she blamed on their unwanted house guest, the poltergeist. No longer able to climb the stairs, she had to sleep downstairs on the settee.

For some reason, this woman unnerved me and seemed to be eyeing us critically, with an almost evil glare. She was openly hostile towards us and was obviously not the person who had requested our visit in the first place. In the middle of our conversation, without warning, she called out loudly for her husband.

"Jim!" she hollered in an extremely masculine and raucous voice that seemed to cause the collection of ornaments, strategically placed across the surface of the sideboard, to vibrate.

"Jim!", she screamed again, ignoring my friend and I completely.

Her husband scuttled quickly into the room, looking somewhat anxious because he had not responded to her call immediately.

"Get me tablets!" she commanded rudely, "and a glass of me sherry."

The little man jumped to attention and disappeared from the room to get the things she wanted.

Throughout the time we spent talking with the woman, I felt as though someone was watching me from behind and I couldn't help turning round quickly to take a look. At this, the woman cackled.

"So, you can feel it too?" she smirked, her eyes suddenly widening with a peculiar combination of terror and glee. "It seems to come from over there!" and she indicated a spot at the other side of the room.

As soon as she spoke, the room went icy cold and I could feel the hairs standing up on the back of my neck.

"What exactly is the problem?" my friend asked Mrs Pritchard. "We were told you have a poltergeist?"

She fell silent and just stared at us with an almost arrogant look on her face.

"Can you explain what exactly has been happening?" I interjected, trying my best to break the uncomfortable silence. "Do things move?"

She began to laugh.

"Move?" she almost growled. "The whole house is alive."

In my experience of poltergeists, I knew full well that the chance of actually witnessing any activity, on any particular occasion, was very slim. However, no sooner had those thoughts passed through my mind, than the door flew fiercely open, nearly smacking my friend in the face. The woman laughed when nobody came into the room.

"You see?" she practically snarled. "The house is bloody well alive. It's infested."

I noticed that at the very moment the door opened, she appeared to be both excited and agitated in some way and I began to wonder whether it was she who was actually responsible for the activity and not a poltergeist.

As soon as my friend turned her attention from the woman to me, a blue vase flew from its resting-place on the window ledge, landing in one piece on the cushion of an armchair. We were both fascinated by the whole scenario and were assured by the woman that the activity we had just witnessed was nothing in comparison to what normally happens.

I had noticed that moments before any paranormal activity took place, she seemed to blank us both out and then fell silent. I was certain that she was to some degree responsible and wanted to explore the phenomenon further. I glanced at the clock on the mantelpiece and noted that it was 4pm and then checked the time against my wristwatch. To my surprise, my watch had stopped at the very time we had entered the house. My friend noticed that her watch had also stopped at the same time. This was beginning to make me feel quite anxious and, at that point, I desperately wanted to get up and leave.

Just as I was about to suggest to my friend that it might be time to depart, the woman's young daughter came home from school. As she entered the room, I saw that she, too, looked pale and sickly, just like her father and it was apparent that her mother paid her no attention at all. She immediately ordered her from the room and when she refused to leave, she smacked her quite hard across the face. The little girl began to sob quite pitifully and then ran from the room.

Because it was getting fairly late, I suggested that perhaps my friend and I could stay one night, some time in the future. Reluctantly, the woman agreed and then we left. We had arranged to stay the following Friday night, primarily because it was more convenient for me. On our arrival this time, we were greeted by Jim's sister, who had requested to speak to us before we entered the room where the woman was lying.

"She's an evil cow!" confided the woman, without any prompting. "Our Jim has had to give up his job to look after her and little Ruth's nerves are in an awful state."

Trying to avoid any involvement in family disagreements, I suggested that we might go into the living at the back of the house. But she pursued us, desperately wanting us to know more.

"You know she's a Romany, don't you?" she whispered under her breath, obviously not wanting the other woman to hear. "She makes things happen just by concentrating. And, she's got a drink problem and drinks with her tranquillisers."

We stayed the night in the same room as the woman and, by midnight, after more than three large glasses of sherry she had fallen into a heavy sleep. This was what I had been waiting for, a chance to see if anything bizarre happened without her intervention. At two o'clock she became quite restless and the coffee table began to shake violently almost at the same time. She began muttering and mumbling in her sleep and she appeared extremely aggressive. The door swung open by itself and the bulb in the table lamp exploded violently. There was a sudden change in the room temperature and a pungent odour once again filled the air.

My friend looked anxiously at me and we both agreed that there was an evil presence in the room. At this point, I was not quite sure whether the woman herself was causing the poltergeist phenomenon to be activated, or whether the poltergeist was having an effect upon the psyche of the woman. Of one thing I was quite sure, whatever it was in the room, it was most certainly evil and I was not too sure whether the woman really wanted it to go away.

I could feel my heart pounding against my ribs as fear coursed through my veins. The curtains began moving, as though being blown by the wind and the vase which had landed safely on the cushion on the previous occasion, crashed loudly onto the floor and shattered into hundreds of tiny pieces. The whole house seemed to be shaking and the pungent odour became even stronger. Chaos reigned for a full 15 minutes and the house, as the woman had so rightly said when we first met her, was alive. Suddenly everything stopped dead and a quiet calm descended upon the house. The woman had slept through it all, probably completely anaesthetised by the sherry and the large meal she had consumed earlier on.

The unpleasant odour gradually gave rise to a sweet fragrance, rather like talcum powder and my friend and I noticed a yellow sheen slowly spreading across the room. Almost at that point, we both saw, clairvoyantly, a middle-aged man walking across the room. He had dark, shoulder-length hair going grey at the temples and he was dressed in a dark suit. He had an olive complexion with piercing dark eyes. He spoke to me and said he had been quite distressed, that he could not move on because his daughter was using up his power and was making herself extremely ill in the process. He revealed that he had died ten years ago and confessed that he was responsible for all her psychological problems.

"I used to beat her when she was a child," he admitted, with apparent shame. "She will not let go of me now and curses me often."

My friend and I realised at once exactly what was causing the paranormal disturbance. She was relying far too much on her husband and child. As long as they were willing to wait on her hand and foot, she would remain on the settee and therefore continue to focus her mind in a malevolent way. She was psychically very powerful and had obviously inherited this power from her father. Because he was constantly on her mind, she was able to draw his energies away from him. There was only one thing for it, her husband and child must move out of the house for a few months.

The following morning we arranged to have a meeting with Jim Pritchard and his sister and my friend and I explained the whole situation as it had been revealed to us and put forward a possible solution.

"It's up to you now," I told him. "If you move away from your wife for a short while, the problem will hopefully be cured. Not only will she recover mentally, but the poltergeist will be eliminated completely from your home."

Jim's sister telephoned me the following day to say that he and his daughter had gone to stay with her for a while and that they had arranged for social services to look after his wife.

Four months later we returned to the house to find the entire atmosphere completely transformed. There was no sign at all of any paranormal activity and the woman had a more positive attitude and had already started to lose weight.

"Would you like a cup of tea?" she asked pleasantly, heaving herself with great effort from the settee, her whole demeanour revealing no trace of the harridan who had greeted us on our previous two visits.

The last time we heard anything, peace and quiet had been restored to the household and Mrs Pritchard had made a full recovery and was working in a sweet shop in Smithdown Road.

The Blind Girl and her Four-Legged Angel

Some stories are often so fanciful and far-fetched that we choose to disregard them completely. But even the most ridiculous story can very often be true. This is one such story concerning a visually-handicapped 28-year-old woman called Rita and how she coped when Fizz, her guide dog, had to be put to sleep, leaving her heartbroken. A large tumour had been found in his stomach and he was in a great deal of pain and, although she had left it for as long as she possibly could, she knew it would be kinder now to let him go.

Fizz had played an enormous part in Rita Fitzgibbon's life for the past 15 years and now she felt as though an important piece of her had just disappeared completely. She missed him so much and would not even consider getting another dog to take his place. Her mother tried constantly to persuade her, knowing the difference a guide dog made to her, just in practical terms but she just could not love another dog as much as she had loved Fizz. Even talking about him made her cry and now she had resigned herself to life without a faithful canine companion.

But, after a lot of persuasion, subtle and otherwise, her mother had eventually brought her to the point of at least considering acquiring another guide dog.

"You do need one, you know, love," she had said and Rita had to admit that she was right.

She was unmarried but lived with her boyfriend, Ron, in Taggot Avenue, Childwall. He worked away quite a lot and so it made sense for her to get another dog.

The first thing on Monday morning the phone rang. It was Mrs Long from the Guide Dog for the Blind Society, ringing to arrange a suitable time to bring Rita her new dog.

"Any time," Rita said, trying desperately to hide her excitement. "As long as you remember that I'm only trying it out for a week or two. I'm not really sure that I'm ready to fill Fizz's place just yet."

Mrs Long said that she fully understood her situation and told her that she would be round that afternoon at two o'clock.

Rita's mother called round to be with her daughter when the new Labrador arrived. She could see that Rita was excited, even though she tried to hide it by making all kinds of feeble excuses about why she did not think the new partnership was going to work.

At 2pm prompt, the doorbell rang. Rita's mother let Mrs Long in with the new dog, which she introduced to her as Jojo. At first she was reluctant to stroke the dog, but she eventually gave in to the temptation when Jojo offered a paw. After the brief introduction, Jojo was left to wander around the house and very quickly became accustomed to where everything was.

Mrs Long visited Rita every day for a whole week and accompanied both her and her new canine friend on their daily walks to the park. Jojo and Rita seemed to work well together and, although he was not Fizz, and could never replace him, it was obvious to Mrs Long that the new partnership was going to work out well.

"He's all yours," announced Mrs Long after the trial period. "Call me if you have any problems!"

Over the weeks that followed their friendship seemed to deepen and their bond became stronger. But then things unexpectedly took a turn for the worse when Jojo suddenly began to do everything wrong. He suddenly became clumsy and allowed Rita to bump into things. On a few occasions he very nearly led her across the road when there was traffic coming. Rita quickly lost her confidence in her guide dog and, as a result, Jojo lost his confidence altogether. Rita just did not know what to do about the situation. Feeling quite despondent and saddened by the whole thing, she reluctantly called Mrs Long.

"I'm quite certain things will improve," Mrs Long tried to reassure Rita. "Why don't you give it one more try?"

Although Rita had lost her confidence completely in her new dog, she reluctantly agreed to try it one more time. After Mrs Long had gone, she sat down and cried. She missed Fizz so much and now she was feeling attached to Jojo and wanted so much for the relationship to work. She prayed that everything would be alright and that tomorrow Jojo would be confident and guide her efficiently.

The following afternoon was a Wednesday and Rita took Jojo for a walk to the Black Woods. This was quite a distance and to get there they had to cross more than one busy road. She was feeling somewhat nervous at first but, to her delight, Jojo behaved remarkably well and did not make any mistakes at all. Her new companion was almost like Fizz and seemed instinctively attuned to all her movements. She was so pleased and smiled contentedly to herself. She would be able keep him now and could not wait to get home to ring Mrs Long and tell her the good news.

On the Friday the vicar called to see Rita and spend an hour with her. He had been out of the country for a while and was now trying to catch up on his job of visiting his parishioners.

"I see you've got two dogs now," he said. "Fizz is still in fine condition considering how old he must be. It's good for him to have a companion. He must feel quite lonely."

At first Rita did not answer and was wondering what on earth he was going on about.

"Two dogs? What do you mean?" she asked.

"I saw you on Wednesday," he said, "walking towards the woods with the two dogs. Jojo was on the lead and Fizz was walking alongside you. He couldn't have been any closer to the pair of you if he'd tried. Fizz seemed to training him."

Rita was suddenly overwhelmed with emotion and she quickly brushed away a tear from her cheek.

"Are you alright?" asked the vicar. "What's the matter? Why are you crying? Have

I upset you?"

Rita turned her face towards him and smiled.

"Fizz is no longer with me," she explained sadly. "He was put to sleep some weeks ago. I've only got Jojo now. He's my baby."

The vicar was lost for words and looked around the room for signs of Fizz.

"But I saw the three of you walking towards the woods," he repeated with a look of bewilderment on his face. "I saw Fizz walking close to Jojo."

Rita reached out and stroked Jojo who was sitting by her chair.

"I'm quite sure you did, vicar," she smiled. "In fact, I know you did. Fizz is now my, no, our, guardian angel."

The Weeping Lady

Most cultures have superstitions, which have been handed down through the ages, involving harbingers of doom and disaster, like the banshee of the Irish tradition. Such beliefs have often been greatly exaggerated and today the superstition of the banshee probably bears no resemblance to the original portentous creature.

The old weeping lady is a figure who makes an appearance in all cultures at times of great misfortune or disaster. However, unlike the banshee, the appearance of the weeping lady is very often a portent of help in a time of great need.

The last recorded appearances of the weeping lady in Liverpool were in 1943, once outside the Philharmonic Pub in Hardman Street and, again, in a Chinese laundry in Myrtle Street.

The Kay brothers had all joined the merchant navy together and had all managed to sign up on the same ship. This was fortunate, as they had been inseparable since boyhood and carried their close bond to the extreme by marrying three sisters. John, Peter and Will had just returned from South America and were making their way to Fong's Laundry in Myrtle Street, to get some shirts cleaned for a dance on the Saturday night. Whenever the three brothers were together, visiting town always meant calling in at several pubs along the way. Their wives reluctantly accepted this and knew only too well that any protestations would fall upon deaf ears.

Out of the three brothers, Peter had the strongest sense of adventure and always seemed to be getting himself into some sort of a scrape. The other two were more cautious and quite level-headed and always had to keep an eye on their younger brother, in case he got himself into trouble.

It was Thursday afternoon and the trio had called into the Philharmonic pub before going to the laundry further along the road. On the way into the pub, John noticed an old lady standing outside the ornate wrought iron gates, crying. She was a frail, pitiful specimen, with a woollen shawl pulled tightly around her tiny shoulders and wrinkled, aged face. Will and Peter had not noticed the woman and carried on into the pub, unaware that John had stopped on the pavement outside. He was just about to approach her, to check if she was alright, when she pointed a crooked, bony finger at him, almost accusingly and so he thought better of it and swiftly followed his brothers inside.

"Where've you been?" asked Will, "You always disappear when it's your round."

"There's an old dear outside crying her eyes out," he said, sounding somewhat upset, "and I went to see if she was alright."

The three brothers soon forgot about the incident and downed a few pints before continuing on their way towards the Chinese laundry in Myrtle Street. As they entered the steam-filled shop, which was owned by the brothers' friend, John noticed the same old woman coming out. She was still crying bitterly and he stood watching her, as she progressed slowly down Myrtle Street, away from city centre. Will came out to see where his brother John was, whilst Peter stayed inside the laundry chatting to his friend, Li Fong.

"What's the matter with her?" asked Will. "Is she alright?"

"Don't know!" John answered. "That's the woman I saw before standing outside the Philharmonic. She's still crying."

As they watched the old woman walking down the street, she stopped and turned to face to the two brothers, then pointed to Will, again, almost accusingly. John looked at Will and frowned.

"She did that to me before!" he said. "She's obviously not all there."

Will laughed as they both turned and went back inside the laundry.

Later on that day, as the three brothers were making their way through town and were just about to catch a bus home, Will saw the old woman again standing outside of the Adelphi Hotel, still crying. He nudged John as they passed her by but, again, Peter was occupied elsewhere and had not noticed her.

The following evening the three brothers decided to take their wives out for a drink and then afterwards into town for a meal. They visited quite a few pubs throughout the evening, but decided to remain in the Willowbank, in Smithdown Road, until last orders were called. The pub was crowded and, by 10pm, everyone in the snug was singing. By the time the three brothers and their wives had left the pub, John, Will and Peter were quite drunk and had to be supported. Peter, as usual, was playing the fool and was trying to walk along the small wall outside the building next-door to the pub. Unable to keep his balance, he fell awkwardly onto the pavement, smashing his head on the wall as he tumbled. He was taken to nearby Sefton General Hospital, where he was kept in for observation.

Over the following few days, the brothers received word that they had to join their ship, The Western Star, in Ireland, from where they would carry a cargo to South America. Because of his accident, Peter was unable to travel and this would be the first time that the brothers had been separated. As Peter had suffered a fairly serious concussion during the fall, he had to spend at least another week in hospital. John and Will said their farewells to him and then left early the following morning for Ireland.

A week later Peter was discharged from hospital. He was extremely impatient to be reunited with his brothers and could not wait for them to return. He knew that they would be away for at least eight weeks and so he arranged a family party for their return. However, on the Friday after Peter was discharged from hospital, the wives of John and Will received some appalling news. Their ship had been torpedoed and there were no survivors. Peter was devastated and overwhelmed with irrational feelings of guilt. He felt that he should have been with them and was somehow convinced that he had let his brothers down. Although he had not actually seen the old woman, Peter remembered his brothers talking about her. He knew now that she was the fabled weeping woman, the legendary harbinger of death, known to point an accusing finger at those who were about to die tragically. If only John and Will had known, thought Peter, they would not have pitied her then.

Shaking Hands with a Ghost

Whether or not it is possible for a ghost to feel solid has often been a point for discussion. Many people claim to have experienced contact with a ghost and have said that it felt as warm and substantial as a living person. Of course, in such cases, it is very rarely realised at the time that contact is actually being made with a ghost. In fact, it is only when the ghostly form actually begins to disintegrate, that it becomes apparent that it is not of this world but of the world of spirits and supersensual beings.

Over the years I have encountered many different kinds of phenomena, from poltergeists to angelic beings floating around the room. However, nothing could have prepared me for what happened on a moonlit night on a country road in Widnes, Cheshire, in 1967.

By the time I left school, in 1962, I had already realised my dream as a professional musician and was touring the country as lead guitarist with my band. Although I had been psychic from a child, my energies during this period were focused in the creative areas of my life as a rock musician and so any psychic experiences which happened, I just accepted as being quite normal for me.

We had been playing at a club in the Liverpool city centre and afterwards had gone for a drink to the now famous Blue Angel in Seel Street, where all the bands in Liverpool in the '60s congregated to unwind after their gigs. We left just after 2.30am and our road manager offered to give two girls a lift home to Widnes.

In the 1960s Widnes was not quite as built up as it is today and it was still very rural in parts. The group's van had been parked at the edge of a country lane and I had walked my friend about 100 yards down the moonlit lane to the house where she lived with her parents. Once I had said goodnight to her and I was on my own, the lane appeared much darker and more eerie than before and I made my way back to the waiting van much more quickly than I had left it.

Upon reaching the bend in the road where I was certain the van was parked, my heart missed several beats when I discovered that it was no longer there. The other guys in the band were forever playing practical jokes on one another and now it looked as though it was my turn to be on the receiving end. But this was beyond a joke. The night was bitterly cold and I was hardly clothed adequately to keep out the biting frost that had already established itself in the November night. I quietly cursed them for leaving me and reluctantly began to make my way down the narrow country lane. The trees cast haunting shadows across my moonlit path and I could physically feel the apprehension and fear creeping all over my skin. My heart began to quicken and I did not know whether to run or hide, having to force my legs to keep moving. My neck began to ache with constantly looking back over my shoulder to check that nobody was following me.

I eventually reached a group of three old cottages, illuminated only by a dim street lamp on the pavement outside and I felt a sudden surge of relief. My steps unconsciously began to slow down as I approached the cottages and the feelings of anger that my friends had deserted me returned, momentarily supplanting my fear.

As I paused by the lamp to quickly scan the lane in case the van had parked where I could not see it, an elderly gentleman appeared, seemingly from nowhere.

"Are you lost?" he asked, in what sounded like a Cornish accent. "Can I be of any help?"

I was a little taken aback to meet such an elderly gentleman so late at night, but he appeared quite friendly and did not give me any cause to be afraid of him.

"No, thanks," I replied, with a noticeable sound of relief in my voice. "I'm making my way back to Liverpool, thanks to my so-called friends."

The elderly man stood in front of me and smiled.

"You'll catch your death wandering about in this weather," he said, reaching out to touch my arm. "You could do with a warm coat on a night like this. I'd ask you in for a warm drink, but my wife is in bed." He gestured towards the end cottage. "I live there. Anyway, I'd better let you go." He reached out and shook my hand and smiled. "My name's Tom Jessop," he added. "Nice to meet you."

His hand was warm and soft and I remember wondering where he had been at so late an hour. He walked through the garden gate and I turned to continue along the moonlit lane. I also wondered if he knew a quicker or more direct way to Liverpool and turned round to ask him but when I looked back, he had disappeared into the house. I could not believe how quickly he had moved, considering his age. I continued to walk along the lane and had gone only a few yards further, when I saw the group's van parked on the road ahead. They had had their bit of fun and I felt so relieved to see them that I decided not to pursue the matter further.

The following day I had to go to Widnes again with Gary, our road manager, on business and we travelled along the same country lane. With no moonlight to cast ghostly shadows, it appeared so different in the daylight. I had told him about the old man and the three cottages and we decided to slow down as we passed them to take a closer look. However, to my surprise, there were now only two cottages and an empty space where the third one had stood the night before. Gary laughed when he saw my puzzled face.

"You must have been mistaken. It was very dark last night."

"But I was standing right outside by the lamp post," I argued. "There were three cottages and the old man went into the first one. He said his name was Tom Jessop."

Gary pulled the van into the curb and we both stepped onto the pavement in front of the two cottages.

"Where are you going?" I called to him, as he opened the gate to one of the cottages.

"I'm going to ask if there has ever been another cottage here," he laughed.

Gary knocked at the door and, within moments, an elderly lady opened it. He made light of the whole thing and practically told the woman that I was crazy and must have imagined the whole episode.

"Oh yes! There was definitely a cottage there," she said, to his surprise. "It was bombed during the War. Mr Jessop and his wife Joan were both killed. He was a lovely man."

"Jessop?" Gary stuttered. "Was his name Tom Jessop?"

"Yes, that's right, Tom Jessop. Your friend's not the first person to have seen him. He suffered from insomnia and used to go for walks at all hours of the night."

Gary was rendered speechless and turned to face me in search of an explanation but I could not believe it either. The old man had shaken my hand and it was warm to the touch. I had definitely seen the cottage with my own eyes and spoken to the old man and yet he was dead and buried and the cottage had long since disappeared. I had actually shaken hands with a ghost.

The Preacher and the Sailor

During the course of my work I hear many strange and unusual stories, none of which has caught my imagination and interest as much as the one you are about to read. I was first told the story of the priest and the sailor by a neighbour, when I was a child and then again when I was in my twenties and it has remained in my memory ever since. The story is quite simple and illustrates perfectly that we should never judge a book by its cover, or a person by the clothes they wear.

It was 1911 and the O'Grady family had just moved into lodgings above a sweet shop in Westminster Road. Tom O'Grady and his wife, Ada, had moved to Liverpool from Dublin with their two daughters, Emily and Mary, six months previously and had been staying with Tom's brother in Manchester until they found somewhere suitable in Liverpool. Although their new lodgings were quite small, they had agreed that they would be adequate until Tom found work. Their landlord had told him about a job on the docks and had promised to recommend him for the position. Tom was not a lazy man and would welcome any kind of work, if it meant keeping a roof over their heads. After a brief interview, he got the job and started work the very next day.

It now looked as though the O'Grady's luck was beginning to change and, to celebrate the occasion, Ada cooked a nice meal for when he arrived home after his first day at work.

Tom had been working at his new job for just over a year when disaster struck. Whilst helping to pack large wooden crates into the hold of a ship bound for the West Indies, he slipped as one of the crates was falling and was crushed to death under its heavy weight. Ada was devastated when she received the news from the dock police sergeant, who called at her home after 10pm that Thursday night. It was doubly sad because it had happened when they were just getting on their feet and had made so many plans for their future.

She had first met Tom when she was only 12 years old and had married him when she was 18. After his death, she felt as though her whole world had fallen apart and now she didn't know what she would do without him.

Although Tom had not been a religious man, Ada herself was a practising Christian and had attended the local church with her daughters every Sunday since moving into the area. Whilst Tom's funeral had been taken care of by the company for which he worked, all that Ada had left of him were their daughters and the clothes he used to wear. He had had no money to leave her and so now she was faced with the sad prospect of a future without a husband to provide for her. She prayed every day for divine help and guidance and for God to send an angel of mercy to help her and her two daughters. Her prayers were obviously a lot more powerful than she realised and were answered within the following month.

One sunny spring afternoon, Ada was sitting by the fire, sadly thinking about Tom. The children were at school and she had never felt so alone in all her life. Suddenly, the sound of the door knocker broke into her thoughts and she wearily rose from her chair to answer it.

Standing on the doorstep was a well-dressed minister of the church, who introduced himself to Ada in a clear American accent.

"John Daynton, from the Good Lord's Temple in Missouri. The Lord has sent me in answer to your prayers. Might I come in to your humble abode?"

At first, Ada thought the caller was crazy and was going to send him on his way.

"Your husband Tom was killed," he continued, raising his eyes heavenward, "and now you are alone with little Emily and Mary and he is with the Lord. You prayed for an angel of mercy to come and help you and now I am here."

Ada was shocked by the preacher's words and, although she still thought him a little strange to say the least, only the Lord Himself could know exactly what she had prayed for. Against her better judgement, she invited the preacher in from the cold.

He seemed to know everything about her whole family, even down to details such as how she and Tom had first met. This made her feel more at ease and she opened up her feelings to the preacher.

"Why are you here?" she asked. "You can't bring Tom back and that's the only thing I want right now."

"No," he laughed, "you are quite right, I cannot bring Tom back to you. But I can give you wealth and comfort for the rest of your life."

"What do you mean?" she said, looking even more confused now. "Give me wealth?"

The preacher rose from his chair by the fire. He retrieved a wallet from his pocket which was bulging with money and placed it on the table.

"This and more," he grinned, dangling it in front of Ada. "You will never have to worry about money ever again."

He sat down once more and crossed one leg over the other, his eyes gazing at her as she sat on the settee by the window. At that moment he made her feel distinctly uncomfortable and she wanted to ask him to leave but his hypnotic eyes somehow prevented her from doing so.

"This all sounds very nice," she said, thinking now that he was some sort of sales person and not a preacher at all, "but I'm really not in the position to make any commitments at the moment."

The preacher grinned and, uncrossing his legs, leaned forward towards her.

"Commitments?" he said in a harsh voice. "The only commitment I want from you is that you accept this money and much more besides, from the one and only Lord."

Although it all seemed so unreal, it was naturally also very tempting to Ada who was penniless, with no prospects of any improvement in her financial state in the foreseeable future. She was beginning to lose her faith, but now she just did not know anymore. With a lot of money, she could at least make a good life for Emily and Mary and herself. As she struggled to decide whether or not to take the money from the preacher, she could feel his eyes boring into her from across the room. Suddenly there was another knock at the door. She checked the clock on the mantelpiece; it was far too early to be the children returning from school. So she asked to be excused and went to see who it was. This time, there was a bearded man standing on the doorstep, with a kit bag slung over his shoulder. His skin was quite tanned and he was dressed rather shabbily and had something of a seaman about him. He had an almost devilish smile on his face as he peered cheekily at Ada.

"I was sent to visit you, my dear, by someone you know very well!" The man's eyes widened, accentuating his round face. "I was told that you are a kind woman and that you would feed me before I set sail again."

Ada could not believe the man's affrontery and began to wonder if he and the preacher were in league together.

"Who sent you then?" she asked, trying to make her voice sound hard and authoritative. "I have no friends."

"Indeed you do," countered the man quickly. "Your husband Tom is still your friend and he asked me to call and speak to you, before you make a big mistake."

Ada was suddenly realised her predicament and felt very afraid and was wondering what on earth she should do. The sailor immediately sensed her fear and smiled reassuringly.

"You needn't be afraid of me," he continued, "and you've every right to think I'm mad. But you must not take any money from that preacher in there."

For the second time that day, Ada was flabbergasted to discover that a perfect stranger seemed to know everything about her.

"How do you know about the preacher?" she whispered earnestly, terrified in case her creepy visitor should overhear their doorstep conversation. "Do you know him? Who is he? Why has he come to visit me?

The sailor rubbed his beard knowingly.

"Indeed, everybody knows the preacher, even you," he grinned. "He's the devil's temptation."

Although she thought the whole scenario was completely absurd and that her two visitors must be totally crazy, she found herself inviting the sailor in from the cold. As soon as he entered the sitting room, the preacher sprang from his chair.

"You should not have allowed this man into your home," he said with a serious tone to his voice. "He is an ambassador of the devil himself."

At this, Ada began to feel very angry and decided that it was time that she took control of the situation. This was her house, after all and she demanded that the two men sit down and listen to what she had to say.

"I might be a vulnerable widow but I am most certainly not stupid." She raised her voice and the two men seemed surprised by her new assertiveness. "Who are you two men anyway?"

The preacher suddenly had a smug look upon his face.

"I am a messenger of the Lord. He has sent me to you," he announced.

"He's lying to you," the sailor grinned. "He is a messenger of the devil himself."

"If that's the case, then who are you?" asked Ada, exasperated. "I suppose you are the messenger from the Lord?"

Before the sailor could answer, the preacher chipped in once again.

"Just take a look at him. Look at the way he's dressed. Do you think the Lord would send a scruffy, unkempt sailor to represent him?" He then gestured to his own clothes. "Look at me and the way I am dressed. I have not come empty-handed like him." He nodded in disgust towards the sailor. "I have brought you money and wealth for the future. The Lord has answered your prayers."

Ada looked at the sailor in search of a response.

"It is true, I have indeed come empty-handed in terms of material wealth," and for the first time he looked solemn, "but I have brought you the gifts of love and support. These will last forever. The money which he has brought you will only bring you tears and loneliness."

By now, Emily and Mary had been delivered home from school by a neighbour and were sitting by their mother, curiously watching the two strange men. Little Emily was feeling unwell and had felt bilious all day at school. Ada's patience was wearing extremely thin and she just wanted to get to the bottom of the crazy scenario which she had found herself in. She decided to propose a simple test to determine which of the two visitors was genuine

"Very well," she announced. "I want you both to sit facing each other and the one who can stare the other out must be the true messenger from the Lord."

"That's an absolutely ridiculous suggestion," scoffed the sailor. "How can that possibly prove anything?"

"You see!" exclaimed the preacher, jubilantly. "He's afraid he'll lose. I agree to the test. When can we start?"

"Remember," said Ada, "whoever moves his eyes first, has lost."

The sailor shook his head.

"This is ludicrous. I have travelled so far to see you. I am tired."

"I have travelled even further," added the preacher, "and I am not in the least bit tired. Surely that must prove something."

The two men faced each other and Ada and her two daughters watched earnestly as the staring contest began. They had only been facing each other for just over one hour, when little Emily fainted and fell heavily onto the floor. Without hesitation, the sailor sprang to his feet and lifted the child from the floor and placed her comfortably on the settee.

"I told you," shouted the preacher. "He's an impostor. I have won."

Ada looked at the preacher without speaking.

"Now do you believe me?" he laughed. "This pitiful figure is an impostor."

Then she looked across at the sailor who was tending her daughter with obvious concern, in contrast to the preacher who was standing there smugly and showing no interest whatsoever in Emily's condition.

"Leave my home this minute!" ordered Ada sharply, gesturing towards the door.

"But I have come to save you from poverty," the preacher pleaded. But when he realised that Ada now knew the truth, his face became cold and unsympathetic.

"You fool!" he snarled. "You absolute fool. You could have had everything."

At that point, the sailor rose to his feet and glared at the preacher.

"Go!" he demanded. "Go and never return to this home."

And, before their eyes, the preacher had evaporated into nothingness, his devilish laughter echoing through the room. She could not believe what she was seeing and, when she turned towards the sailor, he too had disappeared.

From that point onwards, Ada felt reassured that her life was going to change for the better and that she was most definitely still being looked after by Tom.

An Angel Called Rose

This is another story which was related to me during the course of my work.

The grim, old buildings of Sefton General Hospital seemed to conjure up images of poverty and struggle in days gone by. It most certainly had lots of character and when one walked along its endless, dismal corridors late at night, the ghosts of patients long since dead, could be sensed and sometimes heard, calling out from the past.

Harry Walters had been admitted into Sefton General Hospital for a routine check-up and, as there were plenty of beds available, he was put into a side ward all by himself. Harry liked his privacy, so he did not mind being isolated from the other patients. Besides, he knew he would only be in for a couple of days, so it didn't matter to him where they put him, as long as it was quiet. Anyway, since his heart attack, he was quite nervous of any slight twinge that was even remotely connected to this frightening experience. These pains were the reason why he had been admitted on this occasion. He had been in a lot of discomfort and, although the doctor had tried to reassure him that it was not his heart this time, he was quite keen to get a proper diagnosis, to put his mind at rest.

On the Saturday night Harry became quite restless and was finding it very difficult to sleep in the strange hospital bed. He was conscious of the various sounds echoing from the corridor outside his room and the general comings and goings of the night staff. When he checked the time on the clock beside his bed, it was only 3am and so he snuggled down beneath the sheets in a last attempt to get some sleep. He drifted into a light doze, half-aware of the noises outside the room and the more distant sounds of traffic on Smithdown Road, outside the hospital grounds. His pillows were hard and uncomfortable and he became restless once again. He could feel the pain again in his chest and was finding it quite difficult to breathe. He suddenly became aware of someone standing by his bed and he opened his eyes to find a nurse leaning over him, smiling.

"Can I fix your pillows, Harry?" she asked kindly, in a soft Irish voice. "You look quite uncomfortable."

Harry leaned forward whilst the nurse rearranged his pillows and then he sat back and watched her as she walked round the bottom of his bed. He noticed that she was dressed differently from the other nurses, with a somewhat dated appearance. She sat down on the chair beside his bed and spoke to him for a few moments.

"You'll be alright," she reassured him. "It's not your heart this time."

Becoming engrossed in conversation with the friendly nurse allowed Harry's mind to move completely away from his pain and he soon began to feel a little brighter.

"My name is Rose," she told him. "I'm not usually on this ward."

Harry suddenly felt enormously, but pleasantly, tired and before he knew it, the sleep which had eluded him all night, suddenly overcame him.

The following morning he woke up free of pain and feeling completely refreshed. He sat for a few moments thinking about his visit from the nurse in the old-fashioned uniform and wondered who she was. Then, out of the corner of his eye, he noticed something on the locker beside his bed and reached over to retrieve a single red rose. He held it gently between his fingers and sniffed its sweet perfume.

"Rose," he whispered. "Nurse Rose."

Later on that day, after a series of tests, the doctor gave Harry a clean bill of health and told him that he was free to go home the following morning.

Before leaving the hospital, he asked the ward sister about the nurse, describing in detail the way she was dressed and the way she spoke. Before he was able to give her name, the sister interrupted him.

"Nurse Rose," she put in.

"Can I see her before I leave?" asked Harry. "She gave me a great deal of comfort and I'd like to thank her."

"You'd have a job," smiled the sister. "She's a ghost."

"A ghost!" Harry gasped, looking askance at the sister. "She can't be, she sat down next to my bed on this chair. I spoke to her!"

"So have a lot of other patients," she added, quite matter-of-factly. "Her name was Rose Ebison. Apparently she nursed here seventy years ago."

"Seventy years ago?" he repeated, in disbelief. "I can't believe it."

"And I'll bet you felt a lot better after speaking to her?"

"Yes," said Harry, "And ..."

"And," interjected the sister, "she left you a rose."

"Yes," said Harry, his jaw wide open by this time. "How did you know?"

"She leaves everyone a rose," continued the sister. "I suppose it is so that her name is not forgotten."

Harry just could not believe it.

"A ghost left me a rose!"

"No!" smiled the sister. "An angel left you a rose. An angel called Rose."

The Innocent Heart

The congregation had gathered for the Sunday service at St Margaret's and, as it was the main Easter service, the church was completely full. Reverend George Thomson delivered his usual magnificent sermon, once again demonstrating his eloquent oratorial abilities to his attentive flock. He always concluded his sermon with the same meaningful and poignant phrase, "God resides within the heart of everyone". Almost immediately a child's loud sobs could be heard coming from the middle of the church. The vicar paused for a moment whilst the little girl's mother consoled her daughter, but she continued to cry uncontrollably.

Temporarily ignoring the little girl's obvious distress, the vicar brought the service to its conclusion and then immediately wended his way through the congregation to intercept the mother and child as they left the church.

"Is your little girl alright?" he asked, stooping down beside her to offer a comforting arm. "And what's your name?" he asked in a soft voice.

"Rebecca," gulped the little girl.

"What's the matter?" he asked, kindly.

"Oh, she's just being silly," said her mother. "She's alright. Come on, Becky. Stop crying now, you're not a baby."

"I wasn't being silly!" she insisted.

"What is it?" coaxed the vicar. "You can tell me."

She moved her large, innocent, tear-filled eyes to meet his curious gaze.

"You said that God lives in the hearts of everyone?"

"That's right," he confirmed. "He's within us all."

The little girl began to sob again.

"But I've got a hole in my heart."

The vicar was left standing next to her mother, speechless, as she ran off towards the family car.

"I'm so sorry," he apologised. "I'll go and speak to her if you like?"

"No!" said the mother firmly, shaking her head and her own eyes now filling with tears. "She'll be alright. It's just that she's quite poorly. She has quite a few things wrong with her and the prognosis is not good."

"What do you mean?" he continued, concern written all over his face. "Surely her condition can be surgically corrected?"

The woman shook her head solemnly. The hole in her heart can be fixed, but she is also suffering from a degenerative heart condition. Rebecca's consultant has already said that we shouldn't expect her to live any longer than eighteen months - two years if we're lucky."

The vicar was visibly shocked and overwhelmed with sadness for the poor little thing.

"My God!" he said in a low voice. "I'm so sorry."

The woman was overcome with tears and tried desperately to brush them away as she turned to make her way towards her little girl who was waiting by the car.

The following Sunday the vicar looked out for the two of them again but, to his disappointment, they were not at the service. He was a very sensitive and caring man and the little girl's plight had touched him deeply . For the following few weeks, she was on his mind constantly. Then he saw the child's mother at one of the regular Wednesday coffee mornings and he couldn't wait to enquire after her little girl's condition. She seemed equally anxious to talk to him and walked across to him as soon as he entered the church hall.

"Something quite remarkable has happened," she said with an obvious tone of emotion in her voice. "Rebecca was admitted into hospital for further tests. There was no sign of any heart disease at all and, what's even more remarkable, no sign of any hole in her heart. We are all totally amazed and, of course, absolutely delighted."

The vicar was astonished.

"That's quite remarkable!" he said. "I just don't know what to say. I'm so pleased for you."

"It's a miracle!" remarked the woman, "and all because you said that God resides within the heart of everyone."

"And so He does," added the vicar. "This proves that He's most certainly in Rebecca's heart. It is truly a miracle!"

The Little Girl in the Lift

Once people learn what I do for a living, they are only too keen to tell me all their stories and experiences. A recent stay in the Royal Liverpool Hospital was a prime example of this, where I found no shortage of stories and strange happenings.

A porter and a nurse at The Royal Hospital related the following stories to me.

Greg Hamilton had worked at the hospital as a porter for seven years and had experienced many strange happenings during that time. Most of his experiences took place in the dead of night, when there was no one else around and could be explained away, in one way or another, either as the products of his imagination, or as straightforward coincidence. However, what happened to him on the 21 November 1984 was most definitely not a figment of his imagination. He was on a late shift and was not due to finish work until 7am the following morning. Greg did not mind doing the late shift, as there was always something to keep him occupied, ensuring that he never got bored. He had been asked to collect some pillows from a ward on the third floor and, on top of all the other jobs he had to do, he was beginning to feel the pressure. He was way behind with his chores and was rushing as fast as he could to try and catch up with his busier than normal schedule.

The lift doors opened with their usual clang and he stepped in. The lift began to rise again but stopped suddenly at the second floor level. The doors opened and an unaccompanied girl, aged about twelve, entered. Greg was so preoccupied, with all the jobs he had to do, that he never stopped to think what someone so young was doing walking around the hospital, so late at night, on her own.

The lift stopped at the third floor and Greg stepped out into the corridor. He suddenly realised that the little girl was still in the lift behind him and he glanced back to see if she had followed him into the corridor. But the lift was empty and there was no sign of her anywhere.

He told another porter about the experience and he, too, had encountered the same, unaccompanied little girl in the early hours of one November night. Further enquiries revealed that the ghostly apparition had been seen on numerous occasions over the past 20 years and all the descriptions of her corresponded with each other. Even today, she is occasionally still seen and yet nobody seems to know who she is, or where she is going.

The Visitor who Refused to Leave

Although these days hospital visiting times are fairly flexible, up until about ten years ago, they were very strict and limited to one hour per patient, per day, and a restriction of two visitors to a bed at any one time.

Sister Jenkins was extremely conscientious and would always call the visitors to time, dead on the hour. After supper she would make her routine inspection of the ward and when she was quite satisfied that everything was quite in order, lights were out at 9pm prompt. She gave a whole new meaning to the word efficiency and, although she was an extremely hard taskmaster, she was greatly respected by all her staff.

It had been a busy week and Sister Jenkins was feeling quite stressed. Her staff knew what she was like when she was in one of her moods, so everything was done to keep in her good books or, at least, stay out of her way.

When all the visitors had gone and the patients were being settled down for the night, Sister Jenkins marched sternly through the ward and side rooms in typical, sergeant major fashion, checking that all the visitors had gone and that there were no patients slyly sneaking a last cigarette.

As she entered the day room, she noticed that there was a woman, obviously not a patient because she was in outdoor clothes, sitting in the chair in front of the television set, smoking a cigarette. Not only had this visitor broken the rules by remaining after visiting time, but had also left the television set on. Sister Jenkins was outraged and marched boldly past her towards the television.

"Visiting time finished fifteen minutes ago!" she said sharply, turning the television off and spinning round to face the woman.

Her eyes widened in disbelief, however, as she was confronted by an empty chair, in fact, an empty room. The woman had disappeared completely, without even leaving the smell of cigarette smoke behind her. She hurried into the corridor but there was no sign of her anywhere. Sister Jenkins could feel goosebumps erupting all over her body and felt as though someone had just walked over her grave.

"The woman was sitting there in front of the television," she assured herself, "and, as she was elderly, she couldn't possibly have left the room so quickly. Anyway," she reasoned, "I don't believe in ghosts! There must be a rational explanation, but what?"

She was never able to come up with one!

The next story also happened on the same ward and involved two porters who wish to remain anonymous and so their names have been changed for the purpose of the story.

Ron Edwards and Phil Laxton were transporting a middle-aged gentleman from the medical assessment room to a ward capable of treating his illness. Although the man had been brought to hospital as an urgent case, his condition was now stable. As they pushed the trolley from the lift into the corridor, a stern-faced young woman, dressed all in black, passed them to enter the lift. As she did so, she whispered something to Ron Edwards.

"He won't make it to the ward!"

Before he could say anything to her, the lift doors had closed and the woman had completely vanished!

"She's off her head!" he said to Phil in a quiet voice. "Did you hear that?"

"No!" Phil replied, shaking his head. "The look of her was quite enough. She looked like something out of a horror movie."

However, by the time they had reached the ward, to their horror, the patient they were transferring had died of a massive heart attack.

It is said that the spooky woman, dressed all in black, has been seen many times over the years, whispering the same prophetic message into the ear of an unsuspecting porter, as he transports his patient to his, or her, final destination.

The Patient and the Visitor Who Disappeared

Staff Nurse Clare Jones made quite certain that the new patient had been settled down comfortably for the night, before she allowed the woman's husband in to say goodnight.

"You can have fifteen minutes with your wife," she said, "and then I'm afraid I'll have to ask you to leave."

The curtains were still drawn around the bed and so she decided to leave them until the woman's husband had gone. She noticed that there was nothing written on the patient's chart hanging from the end of the bed and, as she had only just come on duty, she had no idea why the woman had been admitted. Before leaving her, she eyed the patient curiously from the end of the bed.

"When were you admitted?" she asked. "This evening was it?"

The woman just stared blankly at the staff nurse and did not seem to understand what she was talking about. So the nurse turned to her husband for an answer but he didn't even look up and just kept staring in his wife's direction.

"Never mind," said the staff nurse, "I'll get someone to check your temperature and blood pressure in a while," and she left the two of them alone.

At the desk, she checked the files for the new patient's records but couldn't seem to find any trace of her.

"What are you looking for?" asked the ward sister. "Can I help?"

"Oh, the patient who was admitted tonight, I can't seem to find her record."

"That's funny," said the sister. "I was looking earlier on. I'd forgotten all about that. I couldn't find them either."

The sister and the staff nurse marched up the ward towards the new patient's bed, not at all prepared for what they were going to find. The sister pulled back the curtains to reveal an empty bed and no trace of either the patient, or her husband. In fact, the bed was still made up and looked completely pristine, as though nobody at all had been in it.

They made a thorough search of the ward and even of the side rooms but there was absolutely no trace of the mysterious patient, or her husband. They had both disappeared without trace. The staff nurse and the ward sister just could not understand it. Who were they and what had they been doing on their ward?

The sister made enquiries at the casualty admission reception, but found that no one had been admitted that night and no new patients had been transferred into ward 2b for the past three days.

Once the story had circulated throughout the hospital, it was found that the ghostly patient and her husband had also been seen in other wards, from where they had also disappeared without explanation.

The Mystery of the Gold Pendant

In the world of the paranormal, there are countless unexplained phenomena, some of which still baffle scientists and psychic investigators today. Objects suddenly appearing, seemingly from nowhere, is one such phenomenon that is quite commonplace in spiritualist parlance. However, to have personal items, such as pieces of jewellery, or even ornaments, spontaneously disappearing for months on end, only to reappear in another place, is not so common a phenomenon. There have been numerous theories about the cause of this unusual sequence of events, most of which have been attributed to mischievous spirits. However, one notable metaphysical scientist said that he believed the cause was simply a transference of energy taking place between one incarnate mind and another.

The following story is true and, to my mind, it completely disproves this scientist's theory altogether. In this case, however, a loving mother, who perhaps wanted justice to be done, produced the phenomenon. I personally have no doubt that discarnate souls can intervene when an injustice has taken place, or when their wishes have not been properly carried out.

Maggie Rowan had nursed her mother until her death, five weeks before Christmas. Although her mother was in her 80s, she was quite young for her years and it was this fact which somehow made it more difficult for her to bear. Maggie's only sister, Jean, was flying over from Los Angeles, where she had been living for the past 20 years. She had planned on staying until the New Year and would help Maggie to clear their mother's house of all her belongings.

Although their mother had very little in the way of money, she did have quite a lot of valuable antiques which had been handed down through the family. Maggie had never been close to her sister, but knew only too well that she would expect to help herself to whatever she liked from her mother's collection. The very thought of this infuriated her. For the last two years both she and her husband, Dave, had looked after her housebound mother, with only the occasional telephone call and letter from her sister. In fact, Jean lived in a different world altogether from Maggie and had always thought of herself as being a cut above the rest of the family. Maggie was mentally steeling herself for her visit and knew only too well that there was bound to be row. Whilst she was quite practical and very down to earth, her sister was extremely materialistic, with the type of personality that had always been quite overpowering.

Jean arrived at Maggie's house quite late on the Friday night and rather than talk about her late mother, she couldn't wait to tell her all about her successful life back in the states.

"I bought this coat in New York," she babbled, insensitively. "You won't believe how much it cost!"

"No," said Maggie, with a completely unimpressed tone and then added, under her breath, "but I'm quite sure you're going to tell me!"

"Just under five hundred pounds."

"My God!" Maggie gasped, unable to help herself. "That's Dave's monthly wage!"

"Oh dear, Maggie! Is that all Dave earns? I just don't know how you manage to make ends meet. And you don't go to work, do you?"

Maggie bit her tongue to hold back her rising anger and frustration.

"Well," she said, bitterly, "in case you've forgotten, I've been looking after mum for the past two years. It would have been a bit difficult!"

"Oh, of course," said Jean, "Sorry, I'd forgotten. But now that mum's gone, though, you can get yourself a little job, can't you?"

Maggie was furious at Jean's callous and uncaring attitude and dreaded the very thought of having her staying for five whole weeks.

Just as she had expected, at Jean's instigation, the house clearing started the very next day. Her eyes nearly popped out of her head every time she found something interesting. However, when Maggie retrieved her great grandmother's gold pendant from the jewellery box and was just about to place it in the drawer, she could see, by the look on her sister's face, that she was determined to have it.

"It is lovely, isn't it?" said Maggie, casually holding it to her neck. "Mother always promised this to me."

"Does it say that in her will?" Jean snapped. "If it doesn't, then I'd like to have it. After all, I am the eldest. It should, strictly speaking, go to me."

"Will, or no will, the pendant is mine," Maggie said firmly, placing the piece of jewellery back into the box. "Let's not forget who looked after mum for two years."

"That's hardly fair!" retorted Jean. "It's not my fault that I live so far away. What could I have done?"

"Whose fault is it, then?" remarked Maggie. "It's certainly not mine. You could have come back to England when I first told you how poorly mum was, at least for a visit."

"You haven't changed, have you?" said Jean, coldly. "You still want everything your own way, don't you?"

"Well, that's rich coming from you! Mum practically begged you not to go to America, but you still went, even though dad had only just died and she really needed your support."

The two sisters spent the entire afternoon in this way, arguing and bickering and trying to score points off each other, until it was quite clear that neither had any love for the other. Thoroughly exasperated, Maggie eventually snatched the gold pendant from the box and flung it onto the bed in front of Jean.

"Here you are!" she screeched. "You have it, if it means that much to you! But you'll never have any luck with it. Mum will make sure of that."

Then she hurried from the room, sobbing uncontrollably, leaving Jean to finish off the job by herself.

For Maggie, the five weeks dragged by with excruciating slowness and, had it not been for the rest of the family volunteering to entertain Jean, she was quite certain that she would not have survived her sister's visit without ordering her to leave.

Apart from the gold pendant and a few other sentimental bits and pieces, Jean returned to America the day before New Year's Eve, with nothing else of her mother's. Maggie was still feeling angry and upset. Although the pendant was not actually mentioned in her mother's will, she knew that she had wanted her to have it and it held tremendous sentimental value for her.

It was the 3 January, Maggie's birthday, and she was polishing the cabinet in the living room to the accompaniment of music from the radio. She was replaying the events of the last few weeks over and over in her mind and feeling quite sad when, suddenly her mother's favourite song came on the radio. The song, Unchained Melody, always made her mother cry for some reason and now it was having the same effect upon Maggie. She stopped polishing and sat down by the fire to listen to it.

When it had finished, she reached over and turned the radio off. She sat for a few moments thinking about her mother and wiping the tears from her eyes with her handkerchief. The silence of her thoughts was suddenly broken by the sound of something clinking inside her mother's blue and white Wedgwood vase, which now stood on the table beside her. Maggie rose from her chair to investigate the source of the noise. Although she knew that the vase was empty because she had recently washed it, she tilted it to look inside. She squeezed her hand through its narrow neck and, to her complete and utter amazement, retrieved from it her mother's golden pendant, which she knew for a fact that her sister had taken back with her to America.

She was at a loss to explain how exactly it had found its way into the vase and wondered whether Jean had suddenly been overwhelmed by feelings of guilt and had perhaps put the pendant there, knowing that their mother had always placed things in the vase for safe keeping. No sooner had this thought passed through her mind, than the telephone rang. To Maggie's surprise, it was Jean.

"I've only just opened the jewellery box and the pendant has gone!" were the first words to greet Maggie's ears. "I just can't understand it, I was looking at it at the airport, before putting it in my handbag. Oh, Maggie, I can't find it anywhere. What do you think can have happened to it? I feel so awful!"

Maggie was astounded by what her sister was telling her but she just smiled smugly to herself and said nothing. She looked down at the beautiful piece of jewellery in her hand and knew for certain now that her mother did want her to have the pendant and had chosen this way to prove it to her from beyond the grave.

"Thanks, Mum," Maggie whispered, clutching the treasured pendant in her hand. "Thanks!"

The Young Man Who Didn't Know that he was Dead

It is believed that when a person dies in tragic, or sudden circumstances, it often takes some time before his, or her spirit, fully realises that it no longer exists in the physical world. Until the realisation comes about that the transition from the physical world has been made, the person has an awareness of two very different landscapes, one superimposed upon the other. This divided consciousness, or state of limbo, only lasts for a very short time, in the majority of cases. However, there are occasions when the deceased person subconsciously refuses to move on, so to speak, and so they still envisage themselves inhabiting a physical body which exists in a physical world. However, the only problem is that nobody in the physical world is actually able to see them.

In my work as a medium and paranormal investigator, I have experienced many such cases of so-called earthbound spirits, when I have had to use my mediumistic abilities to encourage his or her awareness to focus on the supersensual side of their existence. Once this has been achieved, the earthbound spirit 'goes home' quite peacefully, never to return to the physical world again.

This is a true story and one that involves a young man who was killed with his Jack Russel dog in a car crash.

Richard Sharp lived in a flat with his little dog, Snoop, in Livingstone Drive in the Lark Lane area of Liverpool. Although he had many friends, Richard was known to be something of a loner and spent most of his spare time playing with Snoop in Sefton Park. He worked for the Liverpool Parks and Gardens Department and, because he loved being outdoors, he would spend as much time as he possibly could going for walks and drives into the countryside with his four-legged friend. In fact, the two were almost inseparable and, whenever he could, Richard would even take Snoop to work with him, particularly when he was working in nearby Sefton Park.

It was July 1966 and Richard was enjoying his annual two week summer holiday and had decided to drive out to Wales for a couple of days. He liked to paint with watercolours and had decided to take a pad and some pencils with him to make a few sketches of the picturesque countryside. He had it all planned very carefully, just Snoop and himself and the wide-open spaces of the Welsh countryside. He was looking forward to the peace and tranquillity which he thought the two days would bring. However, it was not meant to be.

He had only just set off on his journey, full of pleasant expectation, and had turned right from Parkfield Road into Aigburth Road, when an articulated wagon hit his little car head on, after driving straight through a set of red traffic lights. Both Richard and Snoop were killed outright and his mini car was completely demolished in the impact. As is often the case, the driver of the huge articulated wagon escaped from the accident unhurt.

It was Richard's mother, Mrs Sharp, who contacted me through her friend. She was a staunch Catholic and so consulting mediums was contrary to her beliefs, but she was desperate. She had exhausted all other avenues and I was her last resort.

I called at her home in West Derby on Friday night, just one month exactly after her son had been killed.

"He was a lovely boy," she sighed, as she handed me his framed photograph. "Of course, he wasn't really a boy at all, he was a young man. But he was still a boy to me though."

She began to cry and then sat on the chair by the window overlooking the rear garden.

"He keeps coming to me," she confided, overcome with grief and confusion, "and I really don't know what to do about it."

"What do you mean?" I asked, carefully trying to coax the information from her, without upsetting her even more. "Does he come to you in your dreams?"

"Oh, yes, that too," she answered. "But he comes to me at about six every night." She drew in a deep breath and wiped the tears from her cheeks with her handkerchief. "You see, Richard used to come here every night for his tea. He always had done since leaving home when he was eighteen. He comes each night and sits in that chair crying to me." She indicated the chair in front of the television. "I don't know what to do. Please can you help him?"

I arranged to visit her the following evening just before 6pm. To be perfectly honest, I really thought that her son's appearance was the result of her own emotional trauma and, although I expected to 'see' something mediumistically, I was most certainly not prepared for what was going to happen.

When I arrived, Richard's mother asked me not to sit in her son's chair, as this would be where he would probably appear to us. I must say that I felt extremely nervous and was not at all sure that I would be able to help her. So I sat back in my chair and tried to relax by keeping my mind occupied in talking to her. In the middle of our conversation, I noticed that Mrs Sharp's eyes kept moving backwards and forwards from me to the chair in front of the television. I followed her gaze and noticed a grey mist forming over the contours of the chair. It gradually became more intense and within moments I could see the faint outline of the figure of a man. I couldn't believe what my eyes were seeing and could feel my heart quickening and beads of perspiration forming across my brow. The whole process took no more than one minute and then her son was sitting on the chair facing us. He looked quite solid and I knew that I was not seeing him clairvoyantly, as Mrs Sharp could also see him. I was not mentally prepared for the whole experience and, at this point, I must admit that I felt distinctly alarmed and all my instincts were telling me to leave, but I knew that I could not.

"Richard, love," said Mrs Sharp, gently. "I've brought someone to meet you."

I expected him to respond by turning his eyes to look in my direction, but his gaze remained fixed on his mother. He seemed to be completely oblivious to my presence and appeared to be stuck in some sort of habitual energy stream.

He began to cry and looked pleadingly at his mother.

"What's wrong with me?" he cried.

"Nothing is wrong with you, Richard," she answered in a soft, reassuring voice, her eyes looking to me for support.

"Can I help you?" I asked, as softly as I possibly could. "Please let me help you."

He ignored me completely, seemingly unaware of my presence. I realised then that I had been right in my first assumption and that he could not see or hear me. In fact, Richard was only attuned to his mother's vibrations and so she was the only person who could help him.

He stayed in the chair for at least eight minutes, before finally disappearing in exactly the same way as he had appeared. Although this was an objective paranormal appearance, which anyone present could see, Richard himself could only be aware of his mother and the environment with which he had been so familiar in life.

That night I gave the whole experience a great deal of thought and concluded that there was no way that his mother was going to be able to help her son in the realisation and acceptance that he had, in fact, died. This was likely to be an extremely delicate process and one which had to be handled with great care and sensitivity but also a firm and positive attitude. This, Richard's mother most definitely could not do, as she was far too emotionally involved.

After spending half the night mentally analysing the whole paranormal incident, the answer suddenly dawned on me - Snoop - Richard's dog. Next to his mother, he had been the most important living thing in his life. I knew now what had to be done. The following morning I arranged to call on Mrs Sharp again.

"As you are the only person whom he is aware of," I told her, "you are the only one who can help me."

"Just tell me what to do," she pleaded. "I will do anything to help him find peace."

"When Richard comes to you tonight, you must ask him where Snoop is," I said, hoping that the very question would encourage the dog to manifest itself. "When he becomes aware of the dog, it should persuade him to follow."

Mrs Sharp agreed and I returned to her home just before six that evening. As expected, Richard appeared before us in exactly the same way as before. Mrs Sharp hesitated at first, obviously struggling with her emotions. But then she sat bolt upright in her chair and managed to compose herself sufficiently to address her son in the way in which we had previously discussed.

"Hello, Richard, love, where is Snoop?"

At first he didn't answer and I was afraid that he wasn't going to respond to her question after all. But soon a smile beamed across his face and he repeated the dog's name, "Snoop". Almost immediately, Snoop appeared in front of him, seemingly completely unaware of our presence. The little creature wagged its tail and, without even rising from the chair, Richard disappeared along with his little canine friend. It was as simple and painless as that.

I was not convinced, at that point, that Richard was not going to return the following night and so I told Mrs Sharp that I would ring her at seven o'clock to make sure that everything was fine. As soon as she answered the telephone, I knew that her son had not shown up. I rang her again the following night and still there was no sign of him. Indeed, Richard never returned to his mother's home again after that night. It would seem that Snoop, his faithful canine friend, had taken him home.

The Indian Peg Man

As a child growing up in the mid-1950s, through to the early 1960s, I used to delight in seeing the old Indian man who would occasionally call at our front door, peddling his strange selection of wares, which could be anything from clothes pegs to nylon stockings. A little boy always accompanied the old man and he would just stand beside his father, or grandfather, I was never sure, staring intently at me and my mother, visibly willing her to buy something.

I used to be mesmerised by their exotic appearance. Both the man and the boy wore turbans and the man had a long grey beard, which was twisted at the end into thin, wispy strands. They both looked extremely mystical with their large, brown, hypnotic eyes and had a serene and gentle aura about them.

The man would make a performance of opening up his large suitcase to reveal all his merchandise and was prepared to haggle over the price of the things he was trying to sell. On some of his visits he would mention to my mother that he had some nice clothes for sale, which he had had specially imported from India. At other times, he would suggest that our hall would look nice with a beautiful Indian rug running down its length. He had a very persuasive manner and would very often manage to sell my mother something she did not really need or, for that matter, actually want.

Although the Eastern salesman sold many things, he was, in actual fact, simply known as the Peg Man, primarily because, apart from at our house, pegs were all that he ever seemed to sell in our street.

One day I remember him calling at our house when my mother was feeling a little under the weather. She had not been feeling too well for some time and had even kept me off school for a few days to run errands for her and help about the house. Still in her dressing gown, she opened the door to his smiling and friendly face and I could see that he was immediately overwhelmed by the change in my mother's appearance. He suddenly had a serious look on his face and he placed his suitcase carefully down on the pavement.

"You are not well?" he enquired politely, in a low compassionate voice. "May I give you some medicine prepared from the finest and rarest herbs?"

"No, thankyou," answered my mother politely, "I'm alright, just a touch of the flu I think."

"No," insisted the man. "This is not the flu." He reached out and gently touched my mother's hand. "You have a depression caused by a thyroid deficiency. You must see your doctor as soon as possible."

My mother had great faith in things of this nature and so she did not dismiss the man's advice lightly. So, on the following day, she visited the family doctor, suggesting to her that perhaps her tiredness and depression might be the result of thyroid problems. The doctor made a careful analysis of my mother's systems and then sent her to the hospital for tests. It was some weeks before the results of the tests came back positive. They confirmed that her thyroid gland was underactive and required treatment. This very quickly restored my mother back to her former self and the doctor's prognosis was good. She couldn't wait for the Indian peg man to call again so that she could thank him for his help.

One Thursday I rushed in to tell my mother that he had just arrived at the end of our road and would shortly be at our house. She waited eagerly to greet him and to tell him the news. However, before she could say anything to him he smiled and spoke to her.

"I was correct then?" He scratched his beard and leaned forward. "You are well again. But, unfortunately, your misfortunes are not over yet!"

"What do you mean?" she asked, anxiously. "Is there something else wrong with me?"

The man shook his head solemnly.

"No, but you must tell your husband to take care."

I remember seeing the concern etched on my mother's face as she quizzed him about his doom-laden prophecy.

"Why? What's going to happen to him? Please tell me!"

The man gestured with his hand.

"I see flames by your husband. He must take great care that there is no explosion."

The Peg Man did not even try to sell my mother anything on this occasion, but just turned to walk away.

"Oh! My God!" she gasped, stepping out onto the pavement after him. "He will be alright, won't he?"

The man turned to face her and slowly nodded his turbaned head up and down.

"He will be alright. But he must take care." Then he pointed to the street. "He must take great care."

The man and boy walked away with no further explanation and without even calling at any more houses in the street, leaving my mother and I standing on the doorstep in stunned silence. We watched them until they had turned the corner and had disappeared from sight.

About two weeks later I was playing with my friends in the adjacent road when I noticed clouds of thick, black smoke bellowing high into the air above the houses in my street. My friends and I dashed off to investigate and when we reached the corner of my street we could see that a large crowd had gathered around my father's little van. I could see my mother being comforted by a neighbour and I ran over to be with her. As I approached the scene, I was horrified to see my father lying in the middle of the road, his legs engulfed in flames and the man from next door trying desperately to smother them with an old rug.

Someone had apparently lit up a cigarette whilst chatting to my father, who was about to pour petrol into his van from a can which he had just carried from the local garage. The can of petrol suddenly ignited and apparently my father's only concern was that there were children playing nearby and that the can was going to explode.

He grabbed it and, holding it at arm's length, carried it into the middle of the road, away from the children. His legs caught fire and the lower part of his body but there was no explosion and, because of his quick thinking, a far worse disaster was averted.

I panicked when I saw my father, frightened that he would not survive and wanted to be comforted by my mother but she was lost in her own despair. Within moments, the flames had been extinguished and the ambulance had arrived. Although very shocked and quite badly burned, my father recovered from his ordeal after a short stay in hospital.

Some weeks later, the Indian Peg Man called at our house once more. Before my mother had time to speak, he gave her a reassuring smile and announced that my father was well again.

"I promised you he would be alright, as long as he took care. There was no explosion, that is good!"

When the Indian Peg Man had first issued my mother with that stern warning, he could not possibly have known that my father would try to avoid an explosion, unless he could see into the future.

He continued to visit our street for several years after that incident before his visits suddenly just stopped and we never saw, or heard of him again.

The Vanishing Couple

Most paranormal happenings occur when you are least expecting them. If you watch for them, they very rarely happen. It was once commented to me that we can never be certain, in the sea of faces coming towards us in the city centre on a busy Saturday afternoon, who amongst them is living and who is dead. Ghosts can appear to be quite solid and substantial and may even be quite warm to the touch, as we have seen in previous stories.

This is an account of something which happened to two friends of mine, several years ago, on their return from Southport in the early hours of the morning. Once again all the names have been changed for obvious reasons.

On this particular winter's night, Derek and Barbara McConlon were driving along the Formby by-pass, towards Liverpool, when they came across a young couple, looking frozen stiff, standing miserably at the side of the road, trying to hitch a lift. Normally Derek wouldn't dream of stopping for anyone, particularly so late at night, but Barbara was very persuasive and argued that they looked like nice people and it would be a kind gesture to give them a lift on such a cold night.

So, reluctantly, Derek pulled into the side of the road and the couple clambered gratefully into the back of the car. They thanked Derek profusely and immediately gave their names as Tricia and Dave Egerton. It was November 1969 and the couple said that they had been to a wedding reception in Southport and that they had missed the last train back to Liverpool.

By the time that they had reached the end of the by-pass, on the approach to Ince Blundle, the polite conversation between the four of them had been exhausted and a rather embarrassed silence had descended upon on the car. As they were driving through Ince Blundell, Derek coughed and then asked, "Where can I drop you off?"

His question met with total silence. He thought they must have fallen asleep, so he glanced in the rear view mirror. Upon which, he slammed on the brakes and the car screeched to a juddering halt.

"What's the matter?" gasped Barbara, grabbing the dashboard in alarm.

She had been dozing for the last ten minutes or so and had been jolted awake by the sudden braking movement. She looked across at Derek and was immediately struck by his shocked expression. She turned her head to see what he was looking at through the mirror.

"They've gone!" he stammered in disbelief. "My God! Where are they?"

Barbara climbed out of the car to look back along the road but it was completely deserted.

"I can't understand it!" exclaimed Derek. "They couldn't possibly have jumped out of the car. I was going much too fast. But where the heck are they?"

The incident left the couple more than a little mystified and somewhat unnerved.

They did not know what to think and decided that the whole episode was best forgotten, at least until the following day. By morning their minds would be more rested and better able to make sense of the unusual affair.

The following day was a Sunday and Derek was enjoying his usual lie in, when Barbara suddenly came dashing into the bedroom and spread the morning newspapers on the duvet in front of Derek.

"Look at this!" she said, shaking him awake. "Look at this picture and read the story."

Derek rubbed his eyes and, suddenly noticing Barbara's shocked expression, looked at the newspaper and read the headline:

'Newly Married Couple, Tricia and Dave Egerton, Killed on their Wedding Day in Tragic Accident.'

Who's Nellie?

Telepathy is the phenomenon of mind to mind communication and is the fundamental principle of the process of mediumistically receiving information from the so-called 'dead.' Although we are told that children are far more susceptible than adults to psychic phenomena, when we actually experience a child exhibiting such unusual abilities, it becomes far more credible. The following incident actually happened when my son, Ben, was four years old and obviously extremely sensitive. Although it is never advisable to encourage a child's psychic abilities, there are occasions when one cannot avoid drawing the child's attention to his or her obvious aptitude.

Nellie Baxter was on dialysis for at least three days of the week and, although she was only 67 years old, the quality of her life had deteriorated considerably since I had first met her six years before. Nellie had become almost like a second mother to me and was always there whenever I needed someone to talk to. She had moved into a new council flat in Arundel Avenue and was looking forward to the possibility of a kidney transplant. Even though she was often quite poorly, I never ever heard her complain. I used to visit her nearly every day and would delight in listening to her paranormal experiences over a cup of tea and a Bourbon cream. In fact, whenever I was feeling a little sorry for myself, I would call round to see her for a little consolation. No matter what was wrong with me, Nellie always seemed to put it right with her natural maternal warmth and words of wisdom.

Early in November 1986, Nellie developed an infection and, as a result, suddenly passed away in Sefton General Hospital. Unfortunately I was travelling at the time and so was unable to visit her before she died.

Twelve months later I was driving down Ullet Road, accompanied by my four-year-old son and thinking to myself that if Nellie had still been alive, I would have called in with Ben for a cup of tea. She thought the world of him and always delighted in seeing him when he was a baby, although she had not seen him since he was two years old.

I decided to turn off Ullet Road and drive past Nellie's flat, thinking to myself all the time just how much I still missed her, when Ben, who had been silent all this time suddenly turned to me.

"Who's Nellie, Daddy?" he asked.

I was so shocked that I had to pull the car into the curb.

"What made you ask that, Ben?" I asked, with a somewhat mystified look on my face. During the entire journey I had remained silent with my thoughts and had not mentioned Nellie's name once. He looked at me innocently and declared, "my head was speaking to me!"

"What do you mean, your head was speaking to you?"

Although he is an extremely intelligent lad, I could see that he was unable to explain exactly how he had received this information and simply reiterated what he had first said to me, "my head was speaking to me. It was in my head."

This was obviously a classic example of the phenomenon of telepathy. Ben had not seen Nellie since he was a baby and had never once been taken to her new flat anyway. He could not possibly have remembered her and, even if he had, I hadn't spoken to him about her. If he did not receive her name telepathically from me, then she must have spoken to him psychically. Whatever the explanation, I am quite certain that, on that day, Ben demonstrated a psychic ability by asking me, "who's Nellie?"

Although Ben is now 17 and always dismisses any suggestion that he may be psychic, he had another supernatural experience when he was around the age of five. His mother and I had been divorced for over 12 months and I was missing him terribly. As is often the case in a divorce, there were problems over access and I only saw Ben every month or so.

It was around midnight one Friday night and I was lying in bed, unable to sleep. I was thinking about Ben and feeling quite sorry for myself and silently praying that the situation would soon be resolved. When I eventually fell asleep, Ben came into my dreams and I felt even more depressed when I woke up early the next morning.

The following day I called round to see him at his home near Penny Lane and, to my sheer delight, his mother allowed me to take him out for the day. She told me that during the previous night he had woken up crying and had to be comforted. He told her that I had been standing at the bottom of his bed.

"Your Daddy?" she had said. "You must have been dreaming!"

The very suggestion that he had dreamt the whole thing upset Ben even more.

"No, Mummy, I was awake!" he sobbed. "I saw my Daddy standing at the bottom of my bed."

When I asked her at exactly what time all this had happened, she told me it began around midnight and continued until he finally fell asleep around three o'clock in the morning. This, in fact, was about the time which I eventually fell asleep.

This phenomenon is actually quite common and one that is usually experienced by a person in great distress. When the heart is fretting for a loved one, the incredible release of emotion can cause the consciousness to be transported geographically to that person. The whole experience is charged with emotion and is very often quite realistic and not in any way vague or dream-like.

The Prison Cell Apparition

Alan Rowe was now 56 years old and had been in and out of prison since he was a lad of 18. Since his divorce in 1977, he had made several vain attempts to go straight, but had failed miserably each time, always blaming his background and the influence of his so-called friends. The truth was he was weak-willed and easily-led and did not really want to work for a living. He knew in his own heart now that he would never go straight and just lived his life from day to day, always wishing and hoping that something would happen to improve his circumstances. The strange thing was that Alan Rowe was not the villain whom everyone thought he was. On the contrary, he had a good heart and was always the first to help an elderly person cross the road and even did voluntary work at the local community centre.

Things began to change for Alan Rowe one fateful morning when he prevented two young thugs from mugging 83-year-old Agnes Gill. After fighting off the elderly lady's two assailants, Alan helped the pensioner to her feet and walked her to her front door, just around the corner from where he himself lived. She was so badly shaken that he was reluctant to leave her until the police arrived.

"No, thankyou, I'll be alright," she insisted, declining his kind offer. "You can go now. God bless you, son, and thank you for your kindness. Those people who did this will have no luck. I go to church every afternoon, nothing like this has ever happened to me before. I can see you're a good lad, the Lord will look after you."

The old woman's words touched Alan and stayed with him, making him feel like a fraud when he thought about his past.

A nearby shop assistant had telephoned the police and, within 20 minutes, they had arrived at her home to find the front door swinging open and Agnes lying in the hallway. It was a neighbour who had seen Alan with the old woman and, without knowing the full story, had jumped to the conclusion that he was her assailant. He was subsequently arrested and taken to nearby Allerton Road Police Station and charged with the offence. However, before they even had time to take him to the cells, the desk sergeant received a message to say that Agnes Gill had suddenly taken a turn for the worse and had died of a massive heart attack. The charge facing Alan was now manslaughter and, against his vehement protestations, he was taken to the cells where he was to remain until the following morning.

He was eventually given an eight-year sentence and soon found himself inside Walton Prison. Alan Rowe had now lost all faith in the British judicial system and could not see any point in going on.

Alone in the bare, dismal cell, he felt angry as well as miserable and depressed as he replayed the catalogue of disasters which constituted his adult life, over and over in his tired and confused mind. Although he had brought it all upon himself, he knew that he now had nothing whatsoever to live for. After giving it a great deal of thought, his mind was now made up; he was going to terminate his own life that very night. He had saved a length of twine from the workshop that day and had carefully created a secure knot with a loop large enough to slip over his head. He sat patiently on his bed and waited for lights out, when he could be sure that nobody would find him until the following morning, when it would be too late.

The moment arrived and his cell was plunged into darkness. Alan carefully slipped the noose over his head and tied the end of the twine to his bed. He had thought about it very carefully and had no doubt in his mind that this was the way to do it. By twisting the string tightly around his neck and lying on the floor, he would lose consciousness and be dead within 20 minutes.

No sooner had he secured the noose over his head than he noticed an intense white glow in the corner of the room. It looked as though someone was shining a bright light onto the wall of his cell but, as his eyes became accustomed to the darkness, the glow grew in intensity, eventually taking on the shape of a man with long, flowing garments and shoulder-length hair.

Eventually, the strong light faded somewhat and Alan could see the outline of the man quite clearly. Although he had never been a religious man, he looked just like the biblical figure of Jesus, as he had been portrayed in his childhood bible. He was overwhelmed with a sense of peace and, for a moment, was unable to move. The man communicated to Alan but no words passed from his lips and, in that same moment, the room fell once again into complete darkness.

The following morning Alan woke up with no recollection of having climbed into bed. He searched his cell for the noose which he had made but it had disappeared without trace. In so small and bare a room, this seemed impossible. He could not understand what had happened and began to think that he must have dreamt the whole episode.

That afternoon, the prison governor summoned him to his office and informed him that several witnesses had come forward to testify to his innocence and, as a consequence, he was to be immediately released. He could not believe it. He was a free man again and he shuddered with a mixture of horror and relief when he thought back to the events of the night before.

This time, on his release, his luck began to change. Not only did he feel like a different man but he also seemed to have a completely fresh perspective on life generally. Within a month of being back home, he met a friendly, middle-aged woman and fell head over heels in love with her. He also found a job as a caretaker in a block of flats and, for the first time in his life, he was motivated and able to feel proud of himself. The mould finally seemed to have been broken.

Alan was certain that the old woman whom he had tried to help was somehow guiding him from wherever she now was and that the apparition in the cell was also somehow connected to her. Although he was totally confused by the upheaval in his life, he had also found happiness at long last and now thanked God, and the old woman, for allowing him to find himself - just in time!

Alan Rowe eventually got married to the woman he had met when he was released from prison and now works as a caretaker in a school in Runcorn. He is most certainly not the same man that he was and those who have known him a long time find the metamorphosis very difficult to believe.

The Angel of the Trenches

Bill Gardener had lied about his age to get into the army. It was 1914 and the war had just started and he desperately wanted to be with his 19-year-old brother, Sid, on the front line in France. Although he was only 15 years old, he looked at least 18 and had somehow managed to fool the army recruiting officials and bluff his way through the initial interview. Against his parents' protestations, Bill was on his way to France.

The reality of the war only hit him when he actually set foot on the beaches of France. The smoke-filled air and the constant sounds of exploding mortars overwhelmed him with fear and panic and, for a short while, he almost wished he was back home with his mother and father and younger brother, Sam. But he wasn't, he was in France fighting for his country. Young people find it very difficult to believe in their own mortality but, despite this, every so often it dawned on him that he might even be killed in this war and never see his family again. It was too late now for Bill to change his mind and, although he could already feel the strong camaraderie amongst the other soldiers fighting beside him, in the face of the enemy, it was still every man for himself. Although he had joined up to be with his older brother, as yet, he had not seen him and began to wonder if he ever would.

Sitting in the freezing trenches in the dead of night, Bill tried desperately not to show the others just how terrified he really was. After all, as far as they were concerned he was a man and not a 15-year-old boy, just out of school. Before going to sleep each night he said his prayers quietly, so that the other men could not hear him. He prayed for protection for himself and his brother and asked that they would be delivered safely back home and that the war would end quickly.

Within a few days, the fighting really began in earnest and men of all ages were lying dead and injured in the mud of the trenches all around him. Bill wanted to run but there was nowhere to run to, nowhere hide. He was so frightened and bitterly regretted having lied about his age.

He had been in the trenches for about three weeks and already the fighting was fierce. The incessant noise was deafening and the air in the trenches was so thin and acrid that he could hardly breathe. Suddenly there was a massive explosion and everything went black. He lay unconscious for a long time and came round to a scene of utter devastation. There were bloodied bodies strewn all over the trench and the stench was unbearable. He coughed painfully as he took in a lungful of thick, choking smoke. He struggled to clear his lungs and then fumbled to secure his gas mask on his face and pull himself clumsily to his feet. He felt so weak and could barely move one leg in front of the other, along the slippery duckboards of the trench.

His right leg felt soggy and wet and, judging by the pain in it, he guessed that it was bleeding and that he had sustained some sort of injury in the blast. He managed to make his way carefully along the line of his trench but as far as he could see, all his comrades were either dead or dying. He wasn't sure whether he was lucky to be alive, or whether an even more horrific death lay in store for him. He kept reminding himself that he was only 15 and trying to persuade himself that the Germans simply did not kill 15-year-old boys. But he knew this was not true.

Darkness soon descended and Bill was so exhausted that he made himself as comfortable as he could amidst the slimy chaos of the trenches and fell asleep. Within a few minutes he was woken by the loud cracks of gunfire and harsh German voices calling from no more than ten yards away from the trench in which he was hiding. He quickly pulled himself to his feet and began to move as fast as he could through the darkness. He had no idea where he was heading and was guided only by instinct and sheer terror. He was convinced that he was either going to be killed, or taken prisoner and left to die in some dreadful prisoner-of-war camp. He had never been so frightened in all his life and called out constantly for his brother, Sid.

Just as he realised that the German soldiers had entered the trench and had begun searching the rubble for signs of life, Bill noticed a light shining ahead of him and thought that perhaps one of his comrades had survived the attack and was being careless with his torch. He made his way towards the light and, to his surprise, he could see a young woman dressed in white. She had long fair hair and was carrying a lantern in one hand and beckoning for him to follow her with the other. Bill was afraid that the Germans would also see the light and checked to see if they were following, but there was no one there.

The young woman kept her distance from Bill but stopped every so often to make certain that he was still following her. Although he knew there was a possibility that she was leading him straight to the enemy, instinct alone forced him to keep moving in her wake.

Eventually she rounded a bend where one trench led into another and when Bill had also turned the corner, the young woman had disappeared completely.

He stopped to survey the darkness surrounding him but there was no sign of the young woman anywhere. He could feel his heart pounding hard against his ribcage and was suddenly overwhelmed once again by fear. He felt helpless and completely lost. He fell to his knees in defeat and resigned himself to inevitable capture.

Suddenly, an English voice cut through the darkness and made Bill spring to his feet.

"Where are you?" he cried out in answer. "Keep calling so I can see where you are."

"Over here!" The voice sounded loud and clear. "We're over here!"

Bill moved carefully through the darkness in the direction of the voice and suddenly came upon three wounded men, sitting with their backs to the wall of the trench.

"I'm so pleased to see ..." Bill stopped in mid sentence. "I don't believe it!" he continued, stooping to look more closely at the face of one of the men. "Sid!"

It was indeed Bill's brother who had been calling to him. Apart from having a slight wound on his left shoulder, he was alright. The two brothers had been reunited

123

at last, thanks to the mysterious lady in white, who had guided him with her lantern, through the maze of trenches, to safety.

Bill and his brother were hospitalised for three weeks before returning to the front line. The two brothers were allowed to remain together for the rest of the War and, miraculously, both survived to return to Liverpool in 1918. Although Bill never found out who the lady in the trenches actually was, he never forgot her and always referred to her as the Angel of the Trenches.

The Disappearing Prisoner

Sergeant Frank Taylor took the prisoner to the cells and even made sure that he had one all to himself. After securely closing the heavy metal door, he peeped through the grill to make quite sure that the elderly man had settled down for the night, then returned straight away to his desk at the front of the police station.

The old man had not been charged with any offence, but had simply been found wandering through the streets of Wavertree and brought in to have a night's sleep in the cells. It was the middle of December and it was quite foggy and everywhere was covered with an icy blanket of frost. The constable who had brought the well-spoken elderly gentleman into the station had felt sorry for him being out on such a bitter night and had fabricated a charge, in order to get him a bed for the night.

"Loitering with intent!"

He winked to the desk sergeant who went along with the kindly young policeman.

"Just one night!" the sergeant had said sternly, "Then he'll have to fend for himself, cold or no cold!"

Apart from being bitterly cold, the evening of the 18 December 1948 was a fairly uneventful night at Lawrence Road Police Station, with very few arrests and even fewer disturbances. Around 4.30 in the morning the desk sergeant made himself a cup of tea and broke into the packet of digestive biscuits which he had brought in earlier. He made a cup for his elderly prisoner and emptied a few biscuits carefully onto a plate for him. As he approached the cells, he noticed that there was a sharp draught passing down the corridor and he wondered if the old man had been warm enough in the cell. Before opening the door, the sergeant pulled back the grill to check that he was awake, but the bed was empty and the blankets untouched and still folded neatly at the end.

Somewhat alarmed, the sergeant quickly pulled back the door and peered inside, but the cell was completely empty. The old man was not there and, as there was only Sergeant Taylor himself and two other police officers on duty in the station that night, he wondered which one had allowed him to leave the cell.

On interrogation, neither of the two young constables seemed to know anything at all about the old man being let out of the cell and the sergeant had no cause whatsoever to doubt them. The whole mystery deepened when he checked the entries in his book positioned on the desk at the front of the station. The old man's signature was no longer there!

"But I saw him write it!" he exclaimed. "I watched him. I even remember him saying that he couldn't write properly without his glasses."

Had it not been for the fact that the other constables had also seen the old man with their own eyes and had even witnessed him being taken to the cells, the confused sergeant would have thought that he had imagined the whole thing. However, of one thing Sergeant Taylor was quite certain, the cell door had been securely locked and there was no way that the old man could have got out, unless, of course, he had walked through the walls ...

The Headless Stretcher-Bearer

Most people have heard the phrase, 'running round like a headless chicken!' but very rarely give any thought at all to either its meaning, or, for that matter, where it originated. The fact is that sometimes a chicken's body is able to survive for several minutes after its head has been decapitated. This is a known fact, but what about a human?

John Dunn was a stretcher-bearer in the First World War and had been posted with his best friend, Harry Long, to Belgium. Although they were continuously in the line of fire, neither of the two men was afraid. As far as they were concerned, they were an integral part of an extremely fierce and cruel War and, although they were not required to fire a gun, they were only too aware that their input into the whole War effort was very important.

The two young men had grown up together and it seemed only fitting that they were working together now on the battlefield.

"We'll probably die, together knowing our luck!" John had said jokingly.

However, Harry Long was more philosophical about the whole thing and saw himself as some sort of a hero.

"I don't want to receive my medals for bravery posthumously!" he replied with a serious tone to his voice. "I want to be alive to enjoy all the adulation."

The two friends were inseparable and although they very rarely had any time off, what little time they did have, they spent together in the local hostelry, sampling the local beer. In fact, the War provided them with a great deal of excitement and the thought of being killed by an exploding mortar never seriously crossed their minds.

It was Friday the 13th and the Germans were advancing. Many British soldiers had fallen and John and Harry had been working throughout the night. They had just delivered a wounded soldier to the ambulance, to be transported to the military hospital two miles away, when John was hit in the stomach by a stray bullet. Harry immediately went to his friend's assistance and could see that the wound was serious. As the bullet was deeply embedded in John's abdomen, if his life was to be saved, he would need urgent medical attention. Harry called for another stretcher-bearer to help him carry his friend across the marshy field to the waiting ambulance.

He led the way but they had only travelled a few yards when there was a huge explosion. Harry took the full force of the blast but, without even falling to the ground, the two stretcher-bearers kept on running with John's wounded body. The stretcher-bearer at the rear could not believe his eyes. Harry's head had been blown clean off his shoulders and yet he was still running with his friend on the stretcher towards the ambulance ahead. When they reached it, the stretcher was carefully taken from the two men and Harry was seen to lower himself gently down and to sit with his back to a wooden crate, where he remained absolutely motionless. No one could believe what they were seeing. Even though he had been decapitated, Harry had been determined to save his friend's life and save it he did.

John Dunn's stomach wound had earned him a ticket home and out of the War. His best friend, Harry Long, was buried, along with thousands of other men, on the foreign battlefield where he fell.

The Cat Woman of Toxteth

Very little was actually known about Marie Greer except that she had once been featured on the stages of musical halls all over Britain. Although she was now in her late 80s, she had obviously been an extremely beautiful woman in her day and even now would not be seen in public without looking immaculate. Marie lived alone with her two cats in one of the big Victorian houses in Upper Parliament Street, where she had lived since she was a young girl. Although she was extremely eccentric in both her habits and the way she lived, she was still mentally alert and just as physically mobile as she was when she was 60.

She had never married, this much everyone knew. However, there had been many suitors in her younger days and it was known that she had once been engaged to be married. Her fiancé, however, had been killed in the Second World War and Marie had vowed that nobody would ever take his place.

Marie Greer carried her love of animals to the extreme and could be seen after midnight each night, walking the streets of Toxteth carrying a large basket crammed with cat and dog food. Her route was always carefully planned and although her time often varied each night, her canine and feline orphans were still there in their groups, waiting patiently to be fed.

By day, Marie could be seen going through the same procedure with the pigeons around Granby Street and Kingsley Road and, regardless of what time she came to feed them, they seemed to always know when she was coming and would flock there in their hundreds.

Marie always made a special effort in the winter months and would make two, and sometimes three, feeding visits a day. It was late December 1957 and it looked like it might snow. There was an extremely cold chill in the air and yet the day was bright and clear. On her way to feed the pigeons in Kingsley Road, Marie always popped in to the local newsagents to say hello to the proprietor, Dolly McNally, and to purchase two ounces of imperial creams, her own vice. Thursday was usually a particularly busy day for Marie, as she ended her day with a trip to the Pier Head to feed the seagulls. Dolly was a little concerned as she hadn't been in to see her. She had known Marie Greer for a long time and was only too well aware that there must be something wrong if she had not called in to her shop.

So, as soon as she had closed her shop for the day, she went round to Marie's house. Dolly was forever telling her to sell up and move to something smaller. The house was far too big for one person and only part of it was occupied anyway. But Marie had lived there all of her life and simply refused to leave.

"They'll carry me out in a box!" she had always said to Dolly. "This is my home and this is where I'll stay!"

Dolly got no reply at Marie's home and noticed that the curtains in the front room were still drawn. She felt that there must be something wrong and she quickly returned home and telephoned the police.

The two policemen who called at the house tried knocking and ringing the bell for 20 minutes but failed to get any response. The door was eventually broken open and they were instantly overwhelmed by the pungent smell of cats and dogs. They discovered Marie Greer's body in bed, but were prevented from getting near her by over 30 cats and as many dogs, standing in vigil over her body. Pigeons, too, flew freely around the bedroom and seemed to be trying to prevent any effort by anyone to get near Marie's lifeless body.

The cat woman, as she had affectionately been known, had died naturally in her sleep. Nobody had had any idea of how the old woman had been living. It baffled the police how she had managed to get so many cats, dogs and pigeons into her home and it still remains a mystery today.

The Ghost of Dick Turpin

Such notorious figures as Jesse James, Robin Hood, Al Capone and many others were probably nothing like the legends their names created and yet the stories about their lives still fascinate us today. Many say that Dick Turpin was not the infamous figure we are led to believe he was and that his short life was nowhere near as glamorous and exciting as we are told. In fact, most of what we know about these notorious figures has come to us either directly from the pen of the writer, or the imagination of the Hollywood producer. Although it is not widely known, Dick Turpin visited Liverpool to do business on numerous occasions. He is believed to have stayed in the Lamb public house in the High Street of Wavertree, whilst his horse, Black Bess, was accommodated in the stables.

There are numerous accounts of the ghost of Dick Turpin appearing in various parts of Wavertree and, on several occasions, was said to have been seen around the dock area of Liverpool, where he is believed to have collected merchandise from incoming ships. It is easy to discount these stories by questioning how anyone could know for certain that it was the ghost of Dick Turpin when nobody really knows what he looked like. But, on each occasion, the apparition introduced himself as Dick Turpin and always spoke in a strange, up country accent.

The most interesting account of Dick Turpin's appearance happened in 1940 in Breeze Hill, Bootle, when schoolteacher, Ken Hodge and his wife, Margaret, were on their way home from a wedding reception in the early hours of Sunday morning. Neither Ken nor his wife was inebriated and, although it was in the middle of winter, the weather was fairly mild and the sky clear, revealing a bright crescent moon. When the two were first confronted by the figure in outdated clothes, they assumed it was someone on the way home from a fancy dress party. The fairly diminutive man seemed to appear almost from nowhere as the couple passed the church. He raised his hat to Ken's wife and tilted his head politely, almost immediately drawing a pistol from his belt.

"The name's Dick Turpin," he said in a quiet voice. "I'm so sorry to bother you and your good lady at such an hour, but would you be so kind as to deliver your money into my hands."

No sooner had he spoken than he disappeared before their eyes, leaving the couple quite terrified.

This was no isolated occurrence as he appeared again only a week later. This time it was to a policeman patrolling his beat around the same area. Constable Ernie Clark had just walked in front of the church in Breeze Hill and was standing watching a car passing by. It was just after three in the morning and the police constable was looking forward to the end of his shift. Suddenly, a man in old-fashioned clothes appeared from nowhere and stood boldly in front of the policeman.

"I'm so sorry to bother you," said the strange man. "My name is Dick Turpin, would you please deliver your money into my hands."

Constable Clark also thought that the diminutive man was on his way home from a fancy dress party and smiled indulgently, telling him to get himself home. At that point, the strange figure drew a pistol from his belt, smiled cheekily at the constable and then disappeared right in front of him. The policeman blinked in astonishment. He couldn't believe what he had just witnessed and was sure his colleagues wouldn't believe him. However, he felt compelled to tell someone and when he told his story to another policeman back at the station, he told Ernie that he, too, had encountered the strange apparition.

Research has shown that Dick Turpin did have a young lady in that area and when he visited Liverpool he would call on her. He would always combine his visits to the woman's house with a few hold-ups to make his trip worthwhile and to cover his expenses, I suppose. Of course, it can never be proved whether or not the apparition was really Dick Turpin because, even in those days, well-known figures were often impersonated. I am quite certain that Dick Turpin was no exception and his notorious reputation probably spread all over the country, giving rise to many impostors. The fact still remains that an apparition was seen by many people in the same area.

I Have Been Here Before! (A case for reincarnation)

The Smith family had planned to go to Wales for their annual holiday. In fact, it was the first time they had been to Wales since Kevin was a baby. He was now 12 years old and more able to appreciate the picturesque scenery. Mark was now eight and was also looking forward to the trip. Although he had never been to Wales, he spoke incessantly about the forthcoming holiday with familiarity, almost as though he had been there before. In fact, he chatted so much about Wales that his mother, Joan, had to keep telling him to be quiet. Prior to the holiday being arranged, Mark had never mentioned Wales in his life before. It was almost as though his memory had been jogged in some way, when he was told that the family was going to Wales.

"Kids are like that!" said Peter, his father, passing it all off as childish excitement. "He'll soon change his mind when he gets there and sees how boring it really is."

"You're an old misery!" retorted Joan, whose idea it was to go to Wales in the first place. "Wales is beautiful. Mum and Dad always took us there when we were kids."

"Yeah!" he snarled sarcastically, "and look at them now."

"Don't take any notice of your father," she said to Kevin and Mark. "Wales is beautiful and we'll have a wonderful time."

It was August 1968 and the roads were hectic, with bumper to bumper traffic all along the coast road into Wales. Peter and Joan had expected Mark to talk all the way there but, as soon as they crossed the border into Wales, he fell silent and became almost broody. They had booked a little cottage in an isolated area just outside Gronant, so they were in driving distance of Rhyl, should the kids get too bored and other beaches were not too far away either.

It was an extremely warm and sunny day and the sky was clear without a cloud anywhere to be seen. After they had settled into the cottage and unpacked their clothes, Joan insisted on taking everyone for a walk down the country lane. She wanted to show Peter and the boys the farm she used to visit with her parents when she was a child. For just two shillings they could pick all the apples they wanted and she thought this would be a nice treat for Mark and Kevin if they still did it.

Halfway down the lane Mark started to wander off and when his mother called him, he seemed to be completely oblivious to the sound of her voice.

"Go and see where your brother's going, Kevin," she said. "Bring him back up the lane."

The two boys disappeared over a grassy rise and did not come back for 15 minutes. When they did return, Peter had settled himself down on the warm grass and Joan's patience had begun to wear thin.

"Where have you been?" she snapped. "We were worried about you. Anything could have happened."

"Guess what? Mark is psychic, Mum!" Kevin quipped. "My brother's weird!"

"Why?" said his father. "Have you only just found that out?"

"There's an old mill at the bottom of that hill," Kevin gestured with his head. "Mark knew it was there even before he saw it."

"Don't be stupid!" laughed his father. "He probably saw it before you did."

"He didn't Dad, honest!" Kevin retorted. "He even knew there was a stream behind the mill with an old water wheel."

Joan then noticed Mark's face. It was ashen and he looked as though he was sickening for something. She reached out and felt his forehead.

"What's the matter?" she asked him softly. "Don't you feel too well?"

Mark sulkily pushed his mother's hand away and walked off along the lane.

"I'm alright!" he said. "Are we going?"

Before they reached the farm, about half a mile down the lane, Mark announced that he had been there before.

"Don't be ridiculous!" said his father. "Even I haven't been here before, let alone you."

Joan was anxiously scanning Mark's face and watched his eyes as they seemed to drift off through time. Once again he moved away from the path and began walking towards a stile leading to another large field.

"Where's he going now?" tutted his father. "I'm sure he gets all this from your family. None of my family are weird!"

Joan gestured with her head for Peter and Kevin to follow, as she began moving in Mark's direction. They climbed over the stile and could see their young son standing like a statue, staring thoughtfully across the field.

"What's the matter, love?" she asked, gently placing a comforting arm around his shoulder. "Do you like it here?"

Mark nodded.

"I used to love it when I was a child!"

Peter's eyes shot quickly across to Joan for a response and she could feel a cold shudder pass through her body.

"What do you mean, when you were a child?" she asked, trying to keep her rising sense of panic out of her voice. "What is it that you're feeling? Can you explain it to me?"

"There's a huge old oak tree over there," he answered, pointing towards a gnarled old tree at the far side of the enormous field. "Jesse and I carved our names on it."

He began walking across the field in the direction of the tree.

"What on earth's the matter with him?" hissed Peter, under his breath. "Is he alright? Who the heck's Jesse?"

"I don't know," answered Joan, "He's behaving very strangely!"

They followed Mark across the field and saw that he had stopped by a tall oak tree, and was staring intently at one particular part of it's trunk.

"How uncanny," said his mother. "He was right, here's the oak tree!"

"Don't you start!" snapped Peter. "There's probably at least one oak tree in every field round here. The chances of him being right are very high, don't you think?"

Joan couldn't help but agree with her husband but when they reached the tree where their son was standing, they could see that there was far more to his statement than mere guesswork.

Mark pointed to the trunk of the tree and there it was, just as he had said, two names carved into the centre of a heart. Although now faded and covered with moss and lichen, the two names were clearly visible - Jesse and David.

Peter and Joan could not comprehend the whole affair; their eight-year-old son somehow had a knowledge of a place he couldn't possibly have known about.

"Who are Jesse and David?" asked his mother, by now completely confused by the whole incident.

"Jesse was my girlfriend," he said, sounding quite mature and grown up. "I was David."

Joan's eyes widened in disbelief and she swallowed hard.

"Erm, I don't understand, love," she said in a quiet voice.

She didn't know how to handle the situation and could see that her young son was also more than a little disturbed by the whole experience. She glanced sideways at Peter, in search of moral support, but he had no idea what to do either.

Before Joan could say another word, Mark offered some further information.

"Jesse and I were fifteen years old," he began, with a look of dreamy nostalgia in his eyes. "We had grown up together and promised each other that we would get married as soon as we were old enough."

The couple listened intently to their son's story and found it very difficult to accept that they were hearing the words of an eight-year-old boy.

"We were playing by the water wheel," he continued, "and Jesse's long hair got caught in the wheel as it turned in the water. I tried desperately to save her, but I was pulled down too and we both drowned."

At this point, the little boy began to sob and his mother comforted him.

"Let's go back to the cottage," she suggested, "you need to rest."

Joan and Peter had found it very difficult to find the words to comfort their son. On the one hand, Mark was their child and on the other, he was claiming to have been a 15-year-old boy and a stranger from another time. Joan had read about such matters but had never really given them any serious thought before now. Peter was at a complete loss what to think. Had it not been for the fact that Mark had known about the names carved on the trunk of the tree, he would have put the whole bizarre episode down to his son's imagination. Now, though, he was totally confused and just feared for his psychological state.

Mark insisted that they continue on to the farm and said that he wanted to see if it was the same as before. Joan had forgotten to ask him when it was that he had lived there. It came as a great surprise when he told her that Jesse had lived on the farm and that it was in 1938 when they were both killed.

"That was about the time when I used to visit here with Mum and Dad!" she said, trying to conceal the sudden excitement in her voice. "I used to …" she stopped in mid-sentence when she remembered the girl with long fair hair and her young boyfriend. It all came flooding back to her now and she recalled the reason why she and her parents had stopped visiting the farm. "I remember now," she said to Peter in a low voice. "There was a tragedy, some kind of an accident and Mum and Dad refused to tell me what had happened, in case it upset me."

Silence descended on the four of them as they approached the farm and Joan wondered whether it would still be the same family living there.

"Surely not!" said Peter. "The girl's parents will be well gone."

"But she had two sisters and a brother," she recalled. "Farms are usually kept in the family, aren't they?"

"I suppose so," nodded Peter. "But so what? It won't mean anything to them."

As they approached the farmhouse, a middle-aged man saw them and stopped to greet them.

"Hello there," said the man in a friendly voice. "Can I help you?"

Before Joan could answer him, Mark approached the man.

"Danny, it's really nice to see you."

The man looked at the boy with a puzzled look on his face, then moved his eyes to Joan, thinking that perhaps he knew them.

"Have you been here before?" he asked politely. "Forgive me, your name escapes me. We see so many people, it's quite difficult to remember everyone's name."

Joan could see that the man was uncomfortable and watched his eyes as they kept moving from her to little Mark, who was standing there staring up at him.

Suddenly, unprompted, the man uttered the name, David, in a low voice. Then, shaking his head, he apologised to Peter and Joan, thinking that they wouldn't have a clue what he was talking about.

"Danny!" said Mark staring at the man. "It's me - David!"

The farmer invited the family into the house and they sat and talked about the extraordinary phenomenon. He allowed Mark to take his family on a guided tour of the farmhouse and the child remembered where everything was situated as he led them from room to room. The memories came flooding back to Mark as he showed them photographs of David and Jesse.

"Jesse was my sister," the farmer told them, "and she and David drowned at the old mill, just as your son has told you. This is quite remarkable. No one would believe it, would they?"

The man asked Mark many questions, to which only David could possibly have known the answer. He replied without hesitation, leaving no doubt in the man's mind as to his previous identity. As far as Mark was concerned, there was only one thing missing from the whole bizarre series of events, and that was Jesse herself.

Before the holiday was over, Danny invited the family over to meet his wife and to have a meal with them. They all thought it quite uncanny that young Mark appeared to know more about Jesse than her own family. During the evening it became quite clear to everyone that Mark wanted to find out if Jesse was anywhere in the vicinity and that, if she was, he was obviously determined to meet her before they returned to Liverpool.

There were four days left of the holiday and Mark insisted on staying at the cottage whilst his parents and brother went into the village to collect some food. It was Sunday and everywhere was quiet. Staying in Wales made him feel quite strange and he wasn't too certain about returning to Liverpool at all. He felt as though he was lost in another time and that a part of him was missing. He really did not understand what was happening to him and wanted someone to reassure him that everything would be alright.

He had promised his parents that he would not move away from the cottage until they returned but he suddenly felt overwhelmed with a feeling that he had to go out. He didn't really know where he wanted to go but felt a strong compulsion to go for a walk. He could hear church bells ringing in the distance and decided to head in their direction. He felt a slight rush of excitement in his stomach, as though something momentous was going to happen. He knew that each step he took down the country lane towards the church was out of his control and that he was somehow being guided. He wasn't in any way afraid of the feelings he was experiencing and just allowed himself to go along with them.

When he eventually reached the church, with its grey stone spire reaching up to the blue summer sky, a series of vivid memories overwhelmed him. He used to attend the church with Jesse and they had always promised each other that they would get married there.

Mark stood watching the members of the small congregation going into the church for the morning service. He began to feel a little as though he was waiting for someone to appear, as he checked each face for signs of recognition. Suddenly, he saw a young girl approaching with her mother and she stopped at the gate and stared at him. She looked nothing like Jessie but, nevertheless, seemed to recognise him immediately. She whispered something to her mother and they walked over to Mark. The girl's mother was scrutinising her daughter for some kind of response. At first she didn't speak but just stared deep into Mark's eyes. He felt slightly embarrassed but then the two of them spoke, almost in unison.

"David!" she said in almost a whisper.

"Jesse!"

The girl's mother was obviously aware of her daughter's pre-life experience because she showed no surprise as she watched Mark reach out and gently touch her daughter's face.

"I've found you at last!" he said. "I've waited so long."

Jesse was now Patricia Baldwin and, unlike Mark, had known about her previous life experience since she was very young. Her mother, therefore, understood and helped her daughter all she could. It seemed natural to her that she had been reunited with her one and only love - David.

This is a true story and was related to me, word for word, as it actually happened. Mark is now married to Patricia and they live in Stoke-on-Trent. They are both 47 years old at the time of writing.

The Dwarf Robin Hood of Canning Street

In the early part of the twentieth century, Liverpool was an extremely thriving port and the home of many famous and wealthy people. Most of the Victorian houses in Toxteth today were once the homes of tea and sugar traders, actors, writers and even members of the gentry. In fact, the rich and famous were desperate to buy property in Liverpool and those who were wealthy enough, often boasted of owning more than one home in the city centre. Many would even commute from London to Liverpool, two of the most fashionable places to live in Great Britain at that time.

Number 10 Canning Street was the home of Isaac Barnaby, a wealthy trader and entrepreneur. He was a thoroughly obnoxious man who had very little regard for anyone but himself. Although he was unmarried, his wealth meant that he was never short of a beautiful woman and was always seen on the streets of Liverpool with some of the most fashionable and beautiful debutantes of the day by his side.

Isaac Barnaby employed several servants, one of whom was Richard Dayton, an extremely diminutive figure, standing no more than four feet in height. His behaviour was often described as being most unusual by the other servants, who would occasionally catch him leaving the house after midnight and not returning until the early hours of the following morning. Richard Dayton was an extremely private man and liked to keep himself to himself, often spending his rare days off alone in his small attic room, at the very top of the house.

Richard's best friend was a doctor by the name of Nigel Fimperton, who had a practice in Rodney Street. They had met at medical school and although Richard had also qualified as a doctor, he had become quite disillusioned with the whole medical profession and, as a consequence, had chosen to take time out for a year or two. Thinking that he would like to gain experience of life at a different level, he took a job as the personal valet to Isaac Barnaby. He took an immediate dislike to his new employer and the way he abused his wealth and position. In fact, it was his intense dislike of him which resulted in the birth of Richard Dayton's secret lifestyle, eventually giving him the infamous title of the, 'Dwarf Robin Hood of Canning Street'.

It was 1903 and work had just begun on the new Anglican Cathedral. The city of Liverpool was still in its embryonic stages and was like a volcano on the point of eruption. Nigel Fimperton had always tried to encourage his friend to come and work with him in his lucrative practice in Rodney Street but now Richard had other plans and hoped that he could persuade his friend to join him in his new venture. Richard called in, unannounced, to Nigel's surgery on the Friday night just after five o'clock and insisted that he give him at least ten minutes of his time.

"I have two more patients to see," said Nigel politely, but firmly, "then perhaps you will join me at the club for something to eat?"

Although Richard was quite impatient and obviously very excited by the prospect of what he had to say to his friend, he accepted that he first had to wait until Nigel had finished his surgery.

What Richard had to ask Nigel brought a look of shock and total disbelief to his face.

"I'm a doctor not a burglar!" he exclaimed. "What on earth are you thinking of, Richard?"

He poured two large brandies and sat back on the Chesterfield settee, sipping his drink and eyeing his friend quizzically over the glass.

"Well?" said Richard, raising his brows in amusement. "What do you think of my proposition?"

"I think you are insane," he laughed, sipping at his brandy. "Insane, but I must say the idea appeals greatly to me. I am very tempted!" Nigel sat forward on the settee and raised one eyebrow. "The whole idea is completely absurd!"

"I know!" Richard agreed. "But I know you are like me. That's exactly why I invited you to join me."

"Burglary!" he grinned and sat back in his chair. "Rob the rich to help the poor! Yes, I suppose I can see myself as a modern-day Robin Hood."

The two sat in silence for a few moments, Nigel thoughtfully considering his friend's crazy proposal and Richard watching him patiently for a definite answer. Suddenly a broad grin spread across Nigel's face and he reached over and offered Richard his hand.

"Yes!" he said, with enthusiasm. "Why not? Let's do it!"

Richard Dayton became the 'Raffles' of Liverpool and Nigel Fimperton his associate in crime.

Although forensic science was just beginning to be used, it was still in its innovative stages and so the partners in crime escaped with their booty every time. Richard Dayton's diminutive figure was ideally suited to squeezing through the smallest of windows and nobody was ever any the wiser until after the event.

They burgled some of the wealthiest people in and around Liverpool but only targeted those who were selfish and greedy with their riches. The money they stole was distributed amongst the very neediest citizens of Liverpool, of whom there were thousands and any jewellery they had obtained, was taken to London and sold privately.

The anonymous partnership in crime continued for three years until the two friends were nearly caught in the winter of 1906. Inspector John Kempton had suspected Richard Dayton for some time and had privately declared his suspicions to him. It was this which ultimately brought an end to their partnership. Richard Dayton left Liverpool and went to live in London and Nigel Fimperton continued his life as a respectable doctor in private practice.

Although there have been many legends about the two infamous burglars, they all confirm that they only ever stole from the houses of those who, in their opinion, were selfish and ruthless and abused their wealth and power. They never, ever, harmed anyone during their campaign of wealth redistribution.

It is claimed that Richard Dayton continued his life of crime in London until his death in 1929, at the age of 51. Nigel Fimperton, however, decided to settle for a more sedate life and married a wealthy widow by the name of Jeanette Harding Wolf.

Conclusion

I have always believed that a little knowledge is a dangerous thing where the paranormal is concerned and that great caution must always be exercised when one is dealing with things of this nature. Although over the past ten years great scientific strides have been made in the exploration of the world of metaphysical beings, I do believe that we are no nearer now to understanding the true nature of discarnates and the worlds which they inhabit. Over the last few years or so, I have concluded that very little takes place outside of the human mind.

For example, if I were to take a friend into an old house which I knew to be haunted, but chose not to divulge this information to him, the chances are that he would neither see anything nor sense anything out of the ordinary. On the other hand, if I allowed him to be privy to the knowledge that the house was, in fact, haunted, the spooky scenario would have already been created long before he walked through the door and he would be more receptive to any paranormal activity.

Very few people would actually be afraid to spend the night in a haunted house, as long as they were accompanied by a few friends. But it is a completely different story when we are faced with the prospect of spending the night in such a place alone. The mind creates its own ghosts and demons and is very often able to perceive what is not really there. The truth is that it is in our nature to embroider our experiences and to create scenarios which appear more frightening than they really are. I am quite certain that this is the reason why there is a universal fascination for ghost stories. The process of reading the spooky tale allows the reader to keep a safe distance and to experience the weird happenings at second hand, knowing that at any moment the reality of what is being read can be terminated, simply by closing the book. I suppose this is the great difference between a medium and an ordinary person. A medium possesses the ability to control what he or she experiences and the ordinary person does not.

Fear really only arises from an experience of something which we do not fully understand. The phenomenon of a ghost is very often beyond the normal person's comprehension, especially when somebody else has passed on the ghostly tale to them. However, it is a completely different story when one experiences the ghostly phenomenon at first hand.

Ghosts, too, are very often not all that they seem. One of the biggest misconceptions about ghosts and apparitions is that they are always the spirits of the dead. This is not the case. The majority of paranormal appearances are merely supersensitive images, captured in psychic space. They do not possess intelligence, or even a rudimentary form of consciousness, but are just like a photographic image in the ether.

Everything which possesses the substance of emotion and thoughtpower, is capable of energising its surrounding environment and impregnating it with such intensity as to leave an everlasting impression. These impressions are replayed rather like watching the video of an old movie and are nearly always precipitated by an incarnate mind. There are, of course, the exceptions. Some ghosts are the apparitions of the actual spirit of a so-called 'dead' person who refuses to move on. Very often it is a love of habit which exerts the strongest and most powerful control over a discarnate spirit's life. This is why the old man is often seen sitting in his favourite pub, in the same corner where he always used to sit when he was alive. Or why the lady in white is often seen casually strolling through the garden, following the same route she always took in life. There is an extremely thin veil separating this world from the next and, occasionally, that veil is briefly lifted, allowing us mortals the privilege of glimpsing those things that have been and those things that are yet to be.

Always remember: somebody, somewhere, is watching you!